Fifty Nifty Ways

to
Help Your Child Become a
Better Learner

"Then said a teacher, 'Speak to us of teaching.'"

"And he said:

'No man can reveal to you aught but that which already lies half asleep in the dawning of your knowledge.

The teacher who walks in the shadow of the temple among his followers gives not of his wisdom but rather of his faith and lovingness.

If he is indeed wise, he does not bid you enter the house of his wisdom, but rather leads you to the threshold of your own mind...'"

From <u>The Prophet</u>
Kahlil Gibran

Fifty Nifty Ways

to
Help Your Child Become a
Better Learner

Philip E. Johnson, Ph.D.

Learning to Learn   Tucson, Arizona

This edition was prepared for printing by:

Ghost River Images
5350 East Fourth Street
Tucson, Arizona 85711
ghostriver@gainusa.com

To contact the author please go to:
www.learningtolearn.org

ISBN 0-9749676-0-2

Library of Congress Control Number 2004091390

Printed in the United States of America

Second Printing: July, 2005

10 9 8 7 6 5 4 3 2

Contents

Learning to Learn

Parental involvement in children's learning, both in school and out of school (where most learning takes place!) can make a crucial difference in the children's lives.

But the question is "How?" How can parents be of the most help to their child? The answer to that question is not simple. They can insist that certain hours be set aside for homework, they can attend parent group meetings, they can visit the school and support the child's teacher, they can reward the child for getting good grades, or punish for bad grades, they can be a tutor in American History, or algebra, they can dutifully attend parent-teacher conferences... and it goes on and on.

Some of these are useful, but this handbook suggests a rather different approach.

Simply stated, it suggests that a particularly appropriate role for a parent should center not so much on helping the child to learn the school topics, but rather on helping the child <u>learn how to learn</u>.

Think of education this way - There are two parts to learning. Both are important.

Traditional Education

This aspect of learning is simply the transmission of accumulated knowledge from the past into the minds of the present generation. Almost all of schooling is centered on this theme, and it's extremely important. We are building on the shoulders of giants, all of the learned people of the past. No need to reinvent the wheel. It requires that teachers be experts in their field and nothing could be more appropriate. Imagine a teacher of chemistry trying to teach your high school senior if she didn't know much chemistry! It's the way you and I learned, and over the centuries it has been essentially successful.

But in today's changing world, traditional education has its limitations! For that matter, another name for this kind of schooling is "indoctrination". And thinking stops when indoctrination is the teaching mode. The learner is treated basically as a sponge. Our entire school system is set up to offer and to reward this kind of learning. Better sponges get better grades because they are more able to regurgitate what they "learned". From the perspective of the parent or the teacher, it can be called the "I-know-you-don't-I'm-going-to-tell-you" brand of teaching. And again, it's important, even crucial. But it's not the whole story!!

Learning How to Learn

The other half of the equation, or the other end of the spectrum, might best be called "Learn to Learn". I mean learning the processes of learning, the techniques of learning, the "how" of learning, not only the "what." Learning to be one's own teacher, to translate experiences into assimilated learning . Almost everyone would agree that learning to learn is important, but little is done to directly help students Learn to Learn. We seem to assume that as kids learn the content, they will automatically learn how to learn. Not true. Learning to learn does not happen automatically in the transfer model of education.

But the attitudes, skills, and techniques of learning are eminently learnable and even teachable. They present an excellent opportunity for parental involvement in a child's education. Schools do teach a bit of Learn to Learn, and good teachers always want to do more, but still, on the spectrum of "Learn to Learn" on one end, and "Learn the Content" on the other, schools are much closer to the "learn the content" end.

And for good reasons. There is enormous pressure today, especially in the last several years, on testing, traditional achievement, and good grades. The emphasis is on the content. Working with the concept of L-2-L is difficult. It takes an enlightened teacher who understands deeply how children learn, and how to best support that process. It takes considerable skill in teaching to know how to help kids become motivated and curious, to have them concerned with more than getting the right answer. I said earlier that it would be unfortunate for a teacher of chemistry to try teaching chemistry without knowing much chemistry.

But be aware that it is also very unfortunate for a teacher of chemistry, or anything else for that matter, to teach without knowing much about teaching. Teaching is much more than telling people what one knows.

Helping kids with the processes of learning, that is Learning to Learn, is an excellent role for parents for several reasons.

• We know that kids succeed to a much greater extent if parents are concerned with their learning, care about how they do, and actively support the learning process. A major study many years ago, conducted at Princeton University, investigated the factors that led to kids becoming National Merit Scholars, the very top of the heap academically. "What is it," they asked?" "Intelligence, rural vs. urban, ethnicity or economic status, professional vs. working class parents, parents level of education?" Of all of the variables they investigated, the most telling one was one they called "dinner table conversation." Not limited to the dinner table, of course, this described parents who eagerly asked their kids "What happened in school today?" "What did you do?" What did you learn?" These are the parents who clearly valued learning and made it clear that they cared about their child's learning experiences.

• Supporting the processes of learning is very doable. There are many ways, grounded in enlightened values and attitudes, in which parents can very specifically help their kids to be better at learning. This booklet describes some. Any parent with the appropriate attitudes and values, however, can discover many more. Further, if you have ever shied away from helping your child with a specific homework assignment or other school task because you weren't sure how to go about it, the Learn to Learn emphasis gets you off the hook of having to remember how to do quadratic equations to help your child with intermediate algebra, or remember much about the Civil War to be of help with your sixth grader's Social Studies report.

• Every teacher I have ever known supports the concept of parental involvement in the schools, but many would rather not have the parents directly working with the content. Invariably, however, parents helping kids Learn to Learn is a concept supported by schools and teachers. The parent does not run the risk of interfering or of confusing the child with a different approach than the one used by the teacher.

• By supporting the process of learning more than the specific content, the parent avoids the role of authoritarian, controlling, demanding director, and moves into a much more comfortable role as colleague, supporter, even friend.

• As a result, the parental school role is much happier, more loving than demanding, more obviously caring. And perhaps most important, it's a great way to have fun with your child.

The thesis or theme of this handbook is that learning to learn is crucial, and although supported by schools and teachers, is admittedly not thoroughly addressed in schools.

Further, it is the way that parents can be most helpful to a child's learning both before school begins, in the child's school experiences, and in "out of school" experiences as well.

This handbook will consider the most appropriate role for the school and teachers, the parent, and the child himself in the child's learning. The heart of the handbook is a number of suggestions on how the parent can help the child to become not only learned, but also a lifelong learner.

What This Handbook is <u>Not</u> About.

There are many very important ideas in teaching and learning, all of which can be crucial to a child's success. But this booklet is only about one of them, and in my view, the most important. It is the idea of learning to learn; learning the processes of learning in order to become one's own teacher, and a lifelong learner from one's own experiences. This in no way denigrates the importance of a caring teacher, appropriate and up-to-date curricula, functional facilities, small enough classes, competent and dedicated teachers, and many more. Nor is it a generic criticism of American public education. Most teachers are caring, skillful people, underpaid, operating under difficult circumstances, who totally agree with the need to move toward Learn to Learn, and deserve our support. This booklet is only about how parents can help with learning to learn, a narrow concept, but crucial.

How to Use This Handbook

I suggest that you read the introduction above, and the section "Why Learning to Learn is Crucial". Think about the specific implications of these concepts for you and your child. Skim through the numbered techniques to get an idea of what will come. Many will be difficult to implement, and some will not seem relevant for your child and your situation. **Think about how they can be adapted.** The idea of Learn to Learn seems simple and perhaps obvious, but its implementation can be difficult. It actually represents a major departure from the usual school approach, and especially from the typical pattern of the parents' role in a child's learning.

Be sure to talk it over with your child. Depending on his level of maturity, explain that you want to help but in a gentle way to be a support without being a director. Leave that for the teacher. Suggest that you want to be a "Guide on the Side, not a Sage on the Stage". Ask your child to let you try it out, and to give you some feedback as you go along.

Now read the numbered techniques carefully, adapting each one to your own child, and to your own cultural and emotional situation. Maybe reading just one a day would be a good way to go about it. Most of all, use the numbered idea as a model to develop your own techniques for support of your child. After you read it, develop a little mental "action plan" for use with your child. I've left a space after each numbered issue, with the heading "With respect to this issue, here is what I can do to help my child." Write a few notes to yourself to help you remember, and for later reviewing.

Try to walk the talk; that is, be a model of learning to learn. Learn how to learn yourself, and demonstrate this to your child. As an example, a very good answer to a child's question is "Wow, that's an interesting question, but I sure don't know the answer. How do you suppose we can find out?" Use this handbook to help you discover, and then you can better help your child to discover.

Why Learning to Learn is Crucial

Before we get into the specifics, let's take a look at some of the factors that point to the importance of learning to learn in today's fast moving world.

We are in the midst of the Information Age. The world is changing at a dizzying pace. Consider these issues:

• If an engineer or physician finished medical school or engineering school ten years ago, and has not substantially updated her skills, she is simply out of date. A competent physician needs to know how to learn from her experiences, how to analyze those experiences, and turn them into useful generalizations or theoretical inferences.

• I idly asked my pharmacist a few days ago what percentage of the medications on the racks behind her were not available ten years ago. She thought for a minute, and estimated 80%.

• Some pundit said that the amount of information available to humankind at the time of the birth of Christ doubled by the year 1750. Sounds reasonable to me. It doubled again by 1900, that time taking 150 years to do what previously took 1750 years. Again, this seems sensible. Then another doubling to 1950, again by 1960.... and now, knowledge is doubling about every five years. Doubling!

• Wireless communication, computers...the entire digital world, is changing so fast no one can hope to keep up.

• Our grandparents, maybe even our parents were able to live a lifetime on the information they got in school from the then adequate information transfer system of learning. You and I cannot, and our children certainly can not even approach it. We have to learn from experiences as we go along.

• Adults used to feel completely competent. But now...? Who would not admit to having trouble programming a VCR? Or figuring out how to use the new graphics program we bought for our computer? I have a wireless phone with an 43 page instruction manual!! A telephone!

Other reasons that Learning to Learn is crucial:

When content is presented exclusively as a body of knowledge to be transferred, learners can justifiably conclude that meaning comes from outside themselves. Not true. Real meaning comes from within.

Learning the processes of learning is exciting, and supports additional curiosity rather than merely treating the learner as a passive recipient. We are dealing with "living" wisdom, or understanding, rather than only dead knowledge.

Learning to Learn is dynamic. It carries the seeds of its own transformation.

Simple knowledge can be transferred from teacher to student, but wisdom and understanding result only when the learner "processes" the knowledge. The Learn to Learn teacher or parent supports the student in translating knowledge into understanding.

Tom Friedman, a columnist for the New York Times, describes the schooling of Islamic boys and young men in the Middle East. Taught exclusively by clerics, the teaching style is a classic of learning by transmission only. We call it indoctrination. When they attempt higher education and a professor asks them to think about an issue they have no way to do it. They have never before been asked to think or feel, to solve problems, only to accept what they are told. They therefore revert to even deeper fundamentalism. Would a dictator like a Learn to Learn approach? Not at all. He wants and needs his subjects to be indoctrinated, not to think for themselves. Learn to Learn can be considered education for democracy.

Roles

To summarize the important distinction between traditional, "I-Know-You-Don't-I'm going-To-Tell-You" kind of learning, and a more "Learn to Learn" approach, let's take a look at the roles of the school and teacher, the parent, and the student as they too often are, and as they might become if we move more toward "Learn to Learn".

Schools and Teachers

Schools and teachers are essentially charged with getting the curriculum into the kids. The children need to learn a lot about reading, history, science, mathematics, art and music, and in today's complicated world, much more, often including some very practical vocational preparation. The curriculum, or the content, since we live in a democracy, is determined largely by the schools themselves as a reflection of the needs of society. This can often result in some powerful arguments, as individual families see different needs and have different values in areas such as sex education and religion. Schools want children to come out well on achievement tests. There is evidence of increasing competition among teachers and schools, and among states. Teachers evaluate each child's work and apply letter grades to provide information to parents about how their child is doing, essentially in comparison to the other children.

Teachers are expected, among other things, to be experts in their field, such as science or mathematics, and be able to present material clearly and in a well organized fashion. They must be clearly in control of the class and use appropriate discipline to see that children do what is expected and do not interfere with learning, either their own or the others.

Good teachers also help children to understand their own learning processes, and to become better at learning, but the pressure for content achievement and a proscribed curriculum can not be ignored, nor, of course, should it.

The point of this booklet is that we should all, including teachers, move at least a bit in the direction of Learn to Learn. Transfer learning is important and should not be softened in the move. Fortunately, the two styles are compatible. There is no such thing as learning to learn outside of some content, nor can there be content transmission without at least some incidental Learn to Learn skills being appropriated. But Learn to Learn can and should be much more than incidental.

Children

The youngsters in this equation are too often seen as the passive recipients of the content transmission;

sponges, buckets to be filled with the accumulated knowledge of the past. Better sponges absorb more, if only by rote, and get better grades because they can regurgitate the information at test time. Children are not seen as customers to be asked about their preferences or needs; it is assumed that everyone needs essentially the same knowledge poured in. Children are expected to follow directions, and to be relatively submissive in this hierarchical structure. They are expected to work hard at learning the proscribed curriculum, without having had a voice in its determination. Most of all, kids are not expected to be explorers, discoverers, or even learners. They are expected to become learn<u>ed</u>, which is quite different than becoming a learn<u>er</u>.

Being taught essentially by indoctrination, children become accustomed to someone else being responsible for their learning, not they themselves. They don't learn much about how to learn, since the learning is largely done for them, or perhaps I should say "<u>to</u> them".

The point of this handbook is that children should be seen less as sponges, more as processors of information. They should be given opportunities to explore and discover, to learn how to move from their own experiences, including reading and information provided by teachers and parents, to an analysis of those experiences, and thus to generalizations. Children need to be helped to learn problem solving and creativity; how to "think outside the box".

Parents

The role of today's parents with respect to their offspring's learning is inordinately complex, much more so than in the past. Parents desperately want their kids to be successful, yet find themselves in an ancillary role, subservient to the curriculum centered program at school; outside, looking in. They try hard to motivate and encourage their kids, but still feel as if they are outsiders following the lead of the schools and the teachers. They find themselves in a complex combination of roles; partly teacher, or more likely teacher aide, partly friend and colleague, but partly boss, partly role model.

Single parents have it even tougher! Many working moms come home after a long day at work and find it especially difficult to be supportive of the kids. They need some support themselves!

Parents therefore too easily fall into the role of the one who offers rewards and punishment, the disciplinarian, a behaviorist. They want to avoid at all costs interfering with the curriculum, but to offer appropriate emotional support for their offspring. There are no guidelines. How can we help our children most appropriately, with the right combination of push and pull, the right connection to the school, the right balance between authority and colleague? How to do it well?

Being the coach in a Learn to Learn framework can be an excellent solution to the question of how parents can best support the school and help their children to come as close as possible to attaining their potential. You care about your kids and their future, you want them to do well in school and in life, so accept the role of helping them learn how to learn. It won't interfere with the school curriculum or the teacher's role, and will actually support both. It will help your child to see you as friend and colleague rather than one more authoritarian boss in their lives, and therefore be genuinely motivational. And besides, it's fun!!!

Suggestions for How to Help your Child Become a Learner

Let's consider a few more issues before we get into the specifics.

Like most crucial aspects of a human relationship, the basic values and attitudes are where the behaviors begin. This means that you can't do much in helping your child Learn to Learn unless you have the appropriate attitudes. It's not just a mechanical "follow the dots" kind of program.

One of the basics is that you need to avoid the bossiness or directiveness that too often characterizes the relationship with a child. See yourself as a colleague with your child, so that the two of you together are dealing with the issue. The child then becomes a partner rather than low man on the totem pole. He can feel part of the equation, with a valued voice. This is of course highly motivational. Think of it from your own perspective. If someone, like the boss at work, simply tells you what to do, you might do it, but grudgingly, without much spark. After all, it's the boss' thing, not yours. The same is true for children, of course. The more they feel involved in the decisions that affect them, the more they will be motivated to accomplish something. After all, it's now their thing, not a teacher's or parent's.

Remember also that this business of helping a child is difficult. It's easy to do not enough or too much; to come on too strong, or to be so soft as to be inconsequential. And it will be a new experience for your child. It will take all the skill you can muster to have your child enjoy the climate that you create, to feel successful at learning to learn, and to get recognition from the accomplishments. So keep at it, and try to avoid getting discouraged, especially at first. It's a new deal.

Some of the following suggestions are quite specific, some are more like principles to follow.

Again, you'll have to learn how to make them your own, suitable for your style, your child's style, your child's level of maturity, and your total situation.

1. Get the Focus on Learning as a Process; The "How" of learning

When your youngster comes home from school, ask the usual questions, such as "What did you do in school today? What did you learn?", and be sure to be positive, supportive, even excited about the answer. But try to add the genuine question "<u>How</u> did you learn that?". Have your child identify the learning skill that was used, if possible. Help your youngster to analyze the information he/ she is learning and to come to his/her own conclusions. Questions like "What does that mean to you?", or "Is that something like...?" (Refer to an earlier experience of the child). Be sure you are positive, that you are "up"; pleased that your child knows <u>how</u> to learn things in school. "Wow, that's interesting. You sure have a good teacher! Tell me more about that!".

This is not easy, and will take some time. The first answer you will get to the question "How did you learn that?" is likely to be "The teacher told us". You might point out that this is a very good way to learn, since teachers are usually right, but add to it a question about a related experience, something to use to corroborate the teacher. Or even, for older children and in more sophisticated, less factually oriented situations, to check out the other side of the issue. There are more ways to learn that simply believing the teacher. A competent teacher will surely agree with that position. "And what do <u>you</u> think about it?"

With respect to this issue, here is what I can do to help my child:

2. Asking Good Questions

The one best path to learning is undoubtedly asking questions. There is an art to asking useful questions, too. Your child can ask questions of adults, or maybe even more importantly, of other kids. Get into a dialog with your child about what he/she is learning, and how he/she is going about it. Let your child be your teacher about things the child knows about. Don't fake not knowing, just be sure to ask the child about the information he/she has, and genuinely learn from it. We often learn the most when we teach someone else, so put away your ego or your need to be all-knowing, and illustrate your interest in learning by asking genuine questions of your child. And understand, I'm not talking about asking questions in the way of a test, to see if the child knows. Ask because you want to learn about it. Be proud of being curious, of not knowing, but being interested in finding out. Modeling your own curiosity and skill in asking for information will be one of the most important processes of learning that you can convey.

You can even learn to model asking questions of your and your child's material: books, or the equipment they use in a lab course. Encourage your child to be persistent, not easily satisfied with pat answers, or responses such as "Well, that's just the way it is!" It's your child's learning we're talking about, and it's important.

With respect to this issue, here is what I can do to help my child:

3. Mathematics and Science as Learning to Learn

I have a set of blocks , made in England some years ago, that I have used in workshops for elementary school teachers, to illustrate thinking patterns, and to help teachers to develop curricula and methods to support logical thinking. The blocks are in five shapes, three colors, two sizes, and two thicknesses, making a total of 60 pieces. Many things can be done with them, but one I remember is to put all the blocks in a shoe box, covered, and shake them. Ask the children (or teachers, in this case) what they think is inside. When their guessing gets close, take one piece out for them, not letting them see the remaining ones. Now ask them to ask you for another piece. When they get close, give them another, still hiding the remaining ones. Then ask again. Each time, they will be able to ask a better question. For example, after the thick red circle and the thin blue triangle are out, someone could ask for a thick red triangle. Step at a time, they will learn the attributes of the blocks, and near the end be able to say, "I'd like a thin, small, yellow square". This simple game includes some important parts of logical thinking; the use of set theory, concepts of sorting and relationships of order, equivalence and difference, and the whole idea of inference. Surely there are many other ways to teach mathematics as L2L, rather than the mere accumulation of facts and figures. I realize you can't use the blocks game I described here, but if you have the right attitude, you'll likely be able to turn many learning exercises for your child into an exercise in logic.

You'll be able to think of many other ways to help your child with logic through mathematics. How about figuring mileage on a trip? Connecting the miles with the hours? Given one bit of information, like the price of one pizza, how do you figure out the price of three? Help your child learn to estimate, such as by counting the number of words in several lines of text, averaging, and multiplying by the approximate number of lines to get the total number of words. If you want to leave a 15% tip at a restaurant, have your child figure out how to get the approximate amount. But keep the point on the "how" more than the "what."

Surely a parent's role in relation to science can be in the learning to learn part. Science is a set of skills more than a collection of previously known data. Science is much more than nature study. How about helping your middle school child who is studying biology how to be a biologist rather than just learning biological facts? If you were a biologist, how would you think, observe, organize data? How would you discover new information about plants and animals? What are the tools of the biologist, not only microscopes and taxonomic tables, but what are the thinking patterns a biologist uses? How does a biologist establish an hypothesis? Test it? Draw conclusions? "The Scientific Method" is often a unit in a college science course, but in an appropriate form might well be learned by small children, within the process of leading kids to the excitement of discovery.

Both mathematics and science as a process are wonderfully supported by materials used in Montessori schools. Most teaching supply stores have excellent kits and other materials to help with learning to learn through science and math.

A sixth grade unit in science on which I worked some years ago centered on cultural anthropology. The topic of aggression was included. The sixth graders, using anthropologist's field notebooks, went behind "blinds" set up in the kindergarten, and observed the kindergarten children for instances of aggression and recorded their impressions. Back in their classroom, the teacher led a discussion about aggression. In effect, the sixth graders <u>became</u> cultural anthropologists rather that merely learning already known facts about aggression. And they loved it!

With respect to this issue, here is what <u>I</u> can do to help <u>my</u> child:

4. Model Learning Yourself

Being an adult model of an eager, acquisitive learner is among the most important things we can do as parents. Demonstrate your own curiosity; show that you enjoy discovering new things. Ask questions more than demonstrating that you already know something. And real questions, not just "tests", where you already know the answer. When visiting the zoo, for example, you might say "I wonder what coyotes eat when they can't find mice to catch?" rather than something "lecturey," like "coyotes eat mice, which keeps down the population of mice." I have also found that being a bit tentative is useful. It allows the child to feel respected and to be the parent's colleague instead of subordinate when the parent says "My experience is...; what is yours?" rather than the often cocksure pronouncement.

Be sure to be honest; don't try to fake enthusiasm, don't be "learned." Be curious; not teacher as much as co-learner. Try not to ask fake questions, only real, when you really don't know. Admit that it might be difficult for you. Be a colleague. Show how you figure things out. Look for alternatives. Wonderful conversations with a child begin with the parent saying, genuinely, "What do you think about ...," and then being respectful of the answer.

With respect to this issue, here is what I can do to help my child:

5. Learning Other Than In School

I remember a good experience when I was a Boy Scout, many years ago. We constructed our own transit, using a piece of plywood and a compass, and made a map of our neighborhood. It was fun, I learned about scale and distance, about geometry and geography, and how to read a map, but mostly I learned how to figure things out for myself. There was a lot of involvement on the part of the leader, but it was really an orchestration of the resources, like help in building the transit, suggestions about how to pace off distances, how to ask questions of him and the materials. I learned how to discover the answers rather than expecting the answers from the Scoutmaster.

Be sure that your support of the process of learning is not limited to school work. Most of our learning, especially at an early age, occurs outside of school.

Examples abound - nature walks are opportunities for discovery, there is much to learn from caring for a pet, and camping trips and other family outings provide many learning experiences.

With respect to this issue, here is what I can do to help my child:

6. No Child Left Behind - The Federal Role

Parent involvement in a child's education is powerfully supported by the recently enacted "No Child Left Behind" legislation. Unfortunately, it is sadly underfunded, and at any rate, is not at all consistent with the Learn to Learn side of the equation. Emphasis is on accountability through testing. Testing, however, emphasizes the rote aspect of schools, the "I-Know-You-Don't-I'm-Going-to-Tell-You" portion. Schools compete, based on test scores and those which are losers are labeled as failing. Just like kids, however, schools can't be coerced, but rather must be supported. There is a web site for the program, at www.NoChildLeftBehind.gov which might be of interest to you. "No Child Left Behind: A Parents Guide" provides some information about the program. It is available by e-mail at edpubs@inet.ed.gov or through the web site. A newsletter, "The Achiever", is also available. Sign up for it on the web site. A more relevant site is the FREE site (Federal Resources for Educational Excellence), at www.ed.gov/free. It has a wealth of resources for teaching and learning, including parent tips.

With respect to this issue, here is what I can do to help my child:

7. Rewards

Learning is its own reward. The process of learning is inherently exciting, rewarding. But we seem to get in the way of kids experiencing the fun of learning, the joy of discovery. Make the assumption that learning itself is motivational, and that your child loves to learn. (I'm speaking of learning now, not school. Two different things!) Then identify the ways that we make it demotivating, and eliminate them. And if we need to establish rewards, let's make sure they are applied to the process, the problem solving skills, the "how" of learning, not just the product, the answer. I remember being really appreciative in a statistics course, when the professor gave substantial credit for the correct procedure, even if a mechanical mistake made the answer wrong. I don't mean to say that it's OK to have the wrong answer, but the answer is not the only useful outcome in learning.

The greatest reward for many children is the learning itself, reinforced by an honest appreciative compliment from a parent.

With respect to this issue, here is what I can do to help my child:

8. Grades and Report Cards

I've been convinced for years- as a student, as a parent of four kids, as an elementary school principal, and as a community college and university teacher - that grades are not only useless, but are often counterproductive. They interfere with real learning more than they help. But unfortunately they are a reality.

Listing problems caused by or associated with the grading system is not difficult: grades tend to push students toward competition rather than cooperation, and students begin to function as if the grade rather than the learning is the important outcome. The teacher's control in a hierarchical fashion is supported rather than heading toward a co-learning posture, and learning becomes more a matter of recall and rote. The assumption is fostered that all truth is known and the function of schooling is to transfer it to the mind of the student, rather than learning being a higher level process whereby new information and skills are gained by the student and applied in a useful setting. The very important function of the teacher in providing feedback for the student becomes simplified to the point of being ridiculous, with meaning being vested in one letter, an "A" or "B" or "C". Very clearly and simply, grading gets in the way of learning, especially if by "learning" we mean "learning to learn". Kids don't learn to think "outside the box", nor to value discovery.

At least some of the problem with grading is because schools tend to grade the wrong things- strictly the content: accumulation of facts in math, reading, history, science. What if they forgot about that, and instead graded curiosity, skills in problem solving, asking good questions, ability to put things together, relating earlier learning to new, listening, being one's own teacher, creativity and other skills of learning. Much better! And some schools are making headway in this direction.

Better yet, however, if rather than grading, which is pure evaluation, we learned to provide objective feedback to kids. Objective means non-evaluative information about our perceptions of the kid's performance, leaving the child to do the "evaluating", or adding to it "Gee, I did a good job with that", or "I bet I could do better in the future if I....". Ideas that are self appropriated are more meaningful than those that come from teachers or parents.

Here are a few thoughts about how parents can better deal with grades-

• Minimize the whole thing. It's just not a big deal. Show some interest, but don't let your child feel that the report card is what school is all about, or that grades are the extent of your concern and caring. There are many more important issues.

• Don't reward or punish a child with respect to the report card or grades. Children are subject to behavioral psychology just as much as your pets are, but the more we use external rewards and punishments instead of reinforcing the native joy of learning for the sake of learning, the less effect we will have. Working for the reward, whether it's a ten dollar bill or words of praise, tends to have the child learn for something extrinsic to himself rather than from the pleasure of learning.

• Try to substitute feedback for evaluation. Feedback is non-evaluative, not ending with "Therefore you were good", or worse, "Therefore you were bad". Leave that to the child. Useful feedback might start with words like "I am very proud of you when you..."; or "I noticed that when you ....., the result was....". Make sure the feedback is something under the control of the child, something that he can deal with.

• Don't be comparative, either comparing your child with another, or one reporting period with another, or with yourself at his age.

• Take every chance you get to support the teacher, so that the child is more connected with a sense of personal responsibility. I knew of a parent one time who was negative about the teacher to the extent that the child no longer sensed that learning was her own responsibility. She in effect was saying to herself, "My Daddy thinks that Miss

Martin is not a very good teacher; no wonder I don't do well."

• Keep emphasizing that the important thing is to learn to be a seeker of learning, to be motivated, to be able to solve problems, to figure things out. "Wow, if you keep up like this, you'll get to the point where you don't need a teacher anymore!" (One definition of an educated person is one who no longer needs a teacher; not because he knows it all, but because he knows how to learn).

• Get the child involved in the reporting/grading process. You might ask "How would you have graded yourself if you had filled out the report card?" The purpose of a report card is ostensibly to report to the parents how the child is doing. How about the child reporting too? Frankly, I'd be more inclined to believe the child rather than the teacher if there were a discrepancy. One of the most functional classes I ever taught at a university level was one in which I had the students grade themselves. It freed them to concentrate on learning, rather than satisfying me. I gave up some control so that they could have more control. It worked. Overall, the grades were just a bit lower than what I would have given.

• In any parent-teacher conferences, make sure that the teacher knows that you are concerned about the child's learning to learn processes, not only the accumulation of information as measured by a report card.

With respect to this issue, here is what I can do to help my child:

9. Celebrate Curiosity

Curiosity is the precursor of discovery, and when we can orchestrate the two of them - curiosity and discovery - we have set the stage for impressive learning, and its encompassing concept, learning to learn. Curiosity is foiled by providing ready answers. We should not deliberately withhold information when a question is asked, but go a bit slowly in being the fount of information, which can squash curiosity. Maybe a more measured response could be "That's a really interesting question. Perhaps the answer is that..." Even more to the point of learning to learn would be, if you can be honest about it, "Good question! I've wondered about that too. How do you suppose we could find out?" Or even "My experience tells me that it is... What's your experience with it?"

And be careful to avoid the other side of the "squash curiosity" coin from the ready answer, a response like "Ask your teacher...", or "Go look it up...", or otherwise bypassing it.

Allowing lots of room for your child's views will encourage rather than stifle curiosity. Encourage exploration, trials, mini-experiments on the part of your child. Help with the logic of the thinking process, and praise the process more than the outcome. "You sure went about figuring that out well". Curiosity can certainly be supported, encouraged, and rewarded.

Once again, modeling is crucial. When your child sees you being curious, acknowledging that there are lots of things you don't know but would like to learn, and keeping your own ego and need to be knowledgeable under some control, the more your child will pick up on that and be wonderfully curious herself.

With respect to this issue, here is what I can do to help my child:

Philip E. Johnson

10. Emotions in Learning

Unfortunately, our educational efforts center almost exclusively on the cognitive, the intellect, the brain; thinking. But the feeling world is surely crucial also. The heart contributes enormously to learning. Feelings are an important part of learning, perhaps as important or even more important especially for some, than the cognitive. I was once on a curriculum development team, with the task of developing a new 7th grade Social Studies unit. The purpose was to help kids learn the importance of the division of powers in our constitution: the idea of checks and balances among the executive, legislative and judicial branches. I had learned about this concept in the traditional way in middle school, an American History course in High school, a senior course called "Problems of Democracy", and a college course in history. But it only partially sunk in, not really meaning much to me. The curriculum the team developed included a board game, like Monopoly, in which George III, the King of England, was one player, and members of the English Parliament the others. I was a member of Parliament. Cards were available describing real political moves of the times. The King played a card demanding more taxes for his personal treasury. We objected, so George simply dissolved Parliament! I was incensed! I can still recall the anger. It was unfair, a blatant misuse of power! So I played a card now available to me as landed gentry. I would write pamphlets, trying to stir up the people to resist the King. Next I found myself in jail. I was furious! But to no avail. There was a trial, but the judge was under the control of the king. I was convicted and spent the rest of my life in prison. End of game! But I had learned, through my feelings as well as my mind, that when the Founding Fathers established in the American constitution a provision for the balance of powers, they knew what they were doing, and that knowledge and feeling is still with me!

Some thoughts about the parent role in including emotions in the learning scenario, and thus moving more toward learning to learn.

• When your child is happy and burbling about something at school, reinforce the moment. Join in and say "Isn't it wonderful to feel this way!".

• When asking what was learned and how it was learned, add the question "How did that make you feel?"

• When you read aloud to your child, you have a wonderful opportunity to express feelings. Let your voice and expression carry the feelings of the characters in the book, and ask your child how the character would feel about things.

• When your child tells you about a story, such as in reporting about history or literature, ask how the protagonists must have felt about what was happening. This might be especially relevant when the class your child is telling about included a video or a field trip or even a guest speaker at school.

• Associate learning with a climate for feelings, and acknowledge and respect your child's feelings. It's OK to feel happy or sad or angry over concepts and facts that are being learned.

• Share your own feelings with your child. "I remember being really upset when I was learning about the struggles of the colonists which led to the American revolution."

George Brown wrote an important book some years ago entitled "Confluent Education." By confluence he meant the coming together of the intellectual with the emotional in learning. He included an excellent section where he described teaching Shakespeare with an emphasis on feelings. Learning with and through feelings is an important and neglected area of education, and much related to learning to learn.

With respect to this issue, here is what I can do to help my child:

11. Figure it Out

Encourage your child to figure things out for himself when he is faced with a problem. That's easier said than done, of course, in today's world of high tech equipment and complex technology. But the first step ought to be, when the VCR needs to be programmed, or the term paper needs to be organized, or your teen can't get the computer to do what he wants it to, is to see what he can do about it himself, rather than quickly calling the computer expert or immediately asking you to take care of it. You might ask some questions- like what precisely is the issue or problem, has he ever experienced that before and what did he do then, what is the goal, and brainstorm some possible solutions. Problem solving is a teachable and learnable set of steps, logical patterns, organizational skills and appropriate decision making. Help your child, but control your own ego and don't take over. Your sentences might start with "Have you thought of.....", or What would you think of trying....."

Encourage your offspring to use logic, to think through the steps, to be a detective. Our age of specialization means that sometimes we leave to an expert something we could really do ourselves. There is plenty of need for experts, of course, but have him give it try himself first. He'll gradually get better at solving problems, because he will learn the patterns and develop confidence in his own diagnostic skills. He'll become his own expert. And that's a big step on the road of learning to learn.

With respect to this issue, here is what I can do to help my child:

12. Learning to Learn and Computers

There are generally two rather distinct ways to learn something new, and learning to use a computer illustrates the difference.

One way is the rather traditional method of reading the manual, attending a presentation, taking notes, having instruction from someone who already knows how to use a computer, and in general using your mind exclusively to garner the new information. The learning is cumulative; one bit of knowledge plus another is two, and another bit from the manual or the presentation or the expert makes three.

The other, perhaps no better but just different, involves simply having an experience, such as playing with the machine. "I wonder what happens when I click on this button...??." Then moving from that experience to a higher level, in essence building a theory of how the computer works.

The learning styles illustrate a major difference in learning theory. The first is deductive, that is starting with something general, and deducing the particular instances. The second is inductive, or the reverse, starting with individual instances, like hands-on experiences, and moving toward a more general position. Both are useful, but the inductive is more compatible with the concept of learning to learn. When being inductive, the learner has an experience, like trying something with the computer, then analyzes the experience, such as "Oh, I see. When I click on that button, the computer...". This in turn leads to a self-appropriated generalization, like "Computers.....

When you help your child to be a learner, do your best to be on the inductive side of the equation. For example, the questions might be..."What happened when you tried it?" "What do you suppose that means," or "What can you conclude from that?" The inductive end is especially relevant for a parent, since schools of necessity are heavily into the deductive side.

It also leads to some excellent support procedures on your part, including the sensible question "How did you learn that...," not merely "What did you learn?"

Both inductive and deductive learning are important, both the "how and the "what" of learning are necessary, but the traditional emphasis on the "what" has overshadowed the importance of the "how". As a parent, you can bring these two parts of learning back into balance and help your child to be more of a learn<u>er</u>, not merely learn<u>ed</u>.

Computers are classics of logic, and learning to operate a computer or a new application can illustrate an exciting way to work with your child in the Learn to Learn framework. And since kids almost always love to use a computer, and are very often more technically competent that their parents in doing so, it's also a wonderful framework for developing that all- important relationship with your child where the two of you are colleagues in the learning process rather than you being the boss, and the child being the underling.

More about this inductive-deductive aspect of helping your child later. It's applicable in many situations.

Many adults resent the time kids spend on computer games. Yet the problem solving skills learned with interactive games can be enormous. Computer games can be seen as a classic of moving from the experience to the generalization. Kids can learn directly about logic, patterns of thinking and the like from computer games, and have fun at the same time.

The crucial part, however, often ignored, is that the experience must be "processed-out" to turn it into internalized learning. Here is a wonderful opportunity for a parent. Next time you are being driven crazy by your kid's addiction to a computer game, try joining in instead of fighting it. Try it yourself.

Ask about the game; have your child explain it to you. What are the goals? How do you go about working it? Look for patterns of thinking and point them out to the youngster. "That was really neat, the way you could figure that out!" Making the processes of learning explicit rather than implicit can help them become a part of the child's repertoire of learning, and thus transfer easily to other situations. Next time your child is fussing about not knowing something, you could gently point out that he might transfer the same pattern that he uses when doing a computer game.

A few high-tech suggestions-
• Help your child learn how to search the internet. Not only is there an unbelievable amount of information available, but the logic used in searching is very learnable and important
• Help your child develop his own sense of discrimination about dealing with spam, advertising banners,

objectionable programming, and other computer annoyances and hang-ups.

• Ask your child to show you how to use the VCR or DVD player.

• Have your child help you when the power is off and the digital clocks must be reset.

• Let the impersonal computer be the "expert" in your child's learning, so that the more difficult and important role of "teacher", becomes yours and your child's own role.

With respect to this issue, here is what I can do to help my child:

13. Relationships in Learning to Learn

A functional relationship between your child and his teacher is crucial, and not automatic There is much that can be done to help your child get on well with his teacher, and thus learn, and Learn to Learn, at the optimum.

Teachers are almost universally caring people, who, in a difficult and very underpaid profession, are skilled in helping your child learn. But they have their own needs and their own sense of self, just like your doctor. It's much easier for a teacher to help a child who is curious, eager to learn, and appreciative of the teacher's efforts. When you meet with your child's teacher, ask for advice rather than giving the teacher advice, recognize the teacher's role as difficult, and work with the teacher in a cooperative rather than adversarial framework. Teachers will appreciate it, and in turn do their best to work with your child in the best way possible. They need to feel good about themselves in relation to your child, and be aware that their efforts are functional and appreciated. I don't mean that your child should pander to the teacher, or be overly submissive. You should develop a partnership role with your child's teacher, and help your child to do the same. The child should not be awed by the teacher, nor competitive, but rather should see the teacher as a friend and guide who can be of major help. The teacher's important need to be in control of the class can often be a detriment to the teacher-child relationship, and a child needs to understand that.

Another aspect of relationships in learning is your child's connection with other kids. In order to be "cool" in today's schools, some kids feel that they must be anti-school and anti-teacher. The need for peer support is crucial, especially for adolescents, and can come at the expense of some very important issues. Help your child to find fun in learning, to connect closely with other kids who are also seeking to learn, and in turn model for others an appreciation of learning. Help them develop the interpersonal strength necessary to combat the pressure to be anti-school, and to demonstrate that being a learner can be "cool".

Children can also sense themselves as part of a team, getting help from others. Nothing helps learning so much as teaching the topic, so when your child knows something well, suggest that he help the other kids with it. And when he needs help, other kids are a great resource. One child saying to another, with admiration, "Wow! How did you learn that?" can be almost magic. Wouldn't it feel good to you if someone at work admired you for how you learned something?

In terms of learning to learn, and this booklet, don't forget that the relationship of your child with you is the most important of all. I've said it before, and will again; try to be colleague and friend in the learning process, not the director or boss. Don't be a hero; be democratic.

With respect to this issue, here is what I can do to help my child:

14. Learning to Learn Self-Reliance

A recent column in the New York Times by Nicholas Kristof presented some amazing statistics. Eighty three percent of Americans believe in the virgin birth of Jesus as a literal fact. Only 28 percent believe in evolution. Astrology is used as a guide to decision making by many people. Many people become highly dependent on a psychoanalyst, or a clergyman, a political leader, a parent or a physician. Cult behavior is extensive. Fundamentalism is not limited the fringes of some religions. The importance of a "big daddy " to many people is growing, not diminishing as we might expect as the age or reason matures. I'm not suggesting that we teach our kids to be liberals rather than conservatives, or religious rather than nonreligious, but that we be careful to avoid creating powerful dependency needs in our children. "Is it more important," you might ask yourself, "that my child be just like me, or that he be an independent, self reliant individual, even if we disagree on some issues?" Learn to Learn comes down heavily on the side of self-reliance. The most functional parents guide their children to independence. As I said before, "Be a guide on the side, not a sage on the stage."

A few thoughts about how to go about helping kids to be independent, Learn-to-Learners:

• Provide opportunities for choices, rather than you making the decision. "Would you rather do your homework now or after supper"? Maybe not much of a choice, but it's better than you deciding.

• Discuss the pros and cons of a decision in a 50-50 relationship. Provide data, but allow the child to make the decision to the extent possible.

• When your child decides to be different, on principle, from the rest of the kids, regardless of whether or not you approve of the decision, make sure he knows that you understand and admire the courage it takes.

• Demonstrate your own self-reliance, such as when you take a different political position than a friend or colleague. Then discuss the issue with your child.

• Avoid setting yourself up as "The Expert" in your child's learning. Sometimes the strongest person is the one who is searching for options and exploring both sides of an issue, even to the point of being tentative. Try to be thoughtful rather than "decisive".

With respect to this issue, here is what I can do to help my child:

15. Be a Discriminating Learner

My mother taught me that I should not eat much pepper, because it would give me a heart attack. Plenty of salt was OK though, and lard made pie crust good! Sometimes learning is couched in cultural values or historical information that can be dead wrong. History books tell us that Columbus was a fearless explorer who discovered the New World. Not much is said about his cruelty to the native population. Did you learn that echinacea cures a cold because several generations of Chinese healers have said so? And remember the laetrile craze a few years ago? A chemical extracted from ground-up peach pits was claimed as a cure for cancer.

Sometimes what we learn is from a source that can be deliberately misleading. Did you learn that a particular car was wonderful from the dealer's salesperson, or how great a skin cream is from an ad in a magazine? Advertisers quite naturally want to sell their product, and sometimes cut corners to make their point. A financial planner who also sells securities wears two hats. That's OK, but buyer beware! You might get good advice, but it might be slanted in the direction of the other hat, the one of his making money.

Learning to learn must imply increased discrimination in learning.

How can we help our kids to be discriminating learners, but without being cynical?

The Learn to Learn concept can help.

Often, the question "How do you know that?" is a negative question, really meaning "You don't know what you are talking about!" But stated gently and meant seriously, it can be a useful guide to critical learning.

There are many answers to that question, depending on many variables. One is "'cause my teacher said so!", or "It was in my book" Fair enough, but as kids get to be a bit more sophisticated, it might not really be good enough. Controlled research can be an excellent way of answering questions, but even this can be biased or dead wrong. We are all a bit cautious when a new medication is tested by the pharmaceutical company that developed it and stands to profit from its use.

Perhaps the best way to help your child to be a discriminating learner is to be one yourself, but again, short of cynicism. Judiciously use the question, "How do you know that?" with genuine, honest curiosity, and then help your child to think through the implications. Asking the question often and seriously can help your child to regularly focus on the processes of learning, and become a more discriminating learner.

With respect to this issue, here is what I can do to help my child:

16. Learning About Decision Making and Choices

All of us, as part of being human, are constantly making choices. Some are trivial, such as whether or not to have a second helping of ice cream, and some are important, like whether to move to a new location, apply for a new job, or make a lifetime choice of a partner. Making choices is a learned skill, one which is more than intuitive. We can make good choices, and we can make bad choices.

As a parent, you can help your child enormously to become a self learner by supporting his skills in making choices. Learning the processes of making choices- weighing the alternatives, remembering earlier experiences, seeing what others have done in similar situations -can be of enormous help to a child, especially as he gets older and faces issues like the temptations of drug use, choice of friends, career choices, and the like.

Try not to take a choice situation away from your child by making his decision yourself. If at all possible, see that he is aware that the choice is his, that it could be a good choice or one not so good, and that the consequences of the choice, good or bad, are his, not anyone else's. Unfortunately, many choices that a child can make are taken over by adults, so that the child is denied the learning associated with seeing the results of his own decision. An important parental role is to help the child understand the cause and effect of choices, perhaps by a gentle review. To stay on the positive side, point out positive effects, rather than unfortunate results. For example, "Since you have been hanging out with Carlos, you seem to be doing better in school. You guys are a good team. You made a good decision in being his friend!"

How your child makes these choices is a Learn to Learn issue, and one that most of us neglect in our own lives. Careful decision making can mean the difference between success and failure in many of life's arenas. If we believe that we can determine our own future, that our activities determine the quality of our lives, then it behooves us to plan those activities carefully. As your young child becomes a teen, he will be faced with decisions that have enormous impact on his future. Whether or not to do drugs comes quickly to mind. Help your child realize that his future is very much up to him, not a questions of predetermined fate. What will be is what he makes it. This is the essence of personal responsibility. Help him to learn the processes that he will need to make the best possible decisions.

Your support might initially center on some simple decision, like whether or not to accept an invitation to a social event that conflicts with another desired activity. As the child develops skill in handling simple decisions, the big ones will be easier.

The simplest way to help might be, with your child, to list the advantages of a course of action in one column, the disadvantages in another. Brainstorm as much as you can, then help the child summarize the results and make the decision.

A more sophisticated model you can use to help with planning and decision making is in three stages:
- Assessing the current situation
- Setting goals
- Planning the Activities

Again, a sheet of paper with these headings can guide you both, as colleagues, to make a functional decision. This could be used, for example, to help the two of you decide if the youngster is ready to buy a car, or to go to the nearby community college.

Even more complex, for bigger life decisions, is a procedure called a Force Field Analysis. Based on the work of the social psychologist Kurt Lewin, it is designed to help one look at all the forces surrounding a decision, and plan appropriately.

To do this one, use a sheet of paper with the long dimension top to bottom. Down the center, draw a line, and label the line "The Current Situation". Now draw another line from top to bottom, but this time near the right edge, and at the top label this line "Goal". Now label the left half of the paper, at the top, "Positive Forces", with an arrow pointing to the right. Label the right side of the paper "Negative Forces", with an arrow pointing to the left. It should look like this.

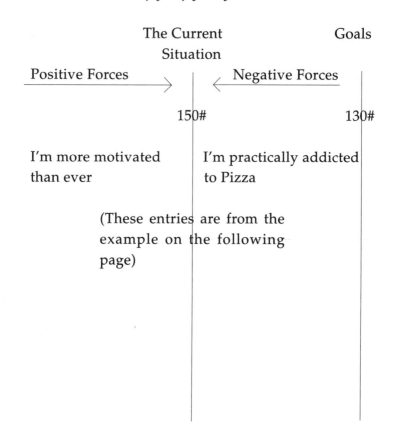

The Current Situation — Goals

Positive Forces → ← Negative Forces

150# 130#

I'm more motivated than ever

I'm practically addicted to Pizza

(These entries are from the example on the following page)

Now, with your child in a partnership and in a tentative fashion, write some aspects of the current situation over the center line. Then determine a goal or two or more, and write them over the right line. A goal is a desired outcome, stated in the future, as "By the end of December, I will have…"

Now comes the interesting part. In the space under the words "Positive Forces" write all the things your child has going for him to move that center line, the way things are, toward the goal. Then list under "Negative forces, everything that seems to be pushing in the wrong way, that is, moving your child from the current situation even further from the goal. Now you have a picture of where you are, where you want to be, and all the things that are helping and hindering.

An example you might visualize is planning for weight control. The center line might be current weight, say 150#. The right line represents the goal weight, let's say 130#. The "Positive Forces " column might include things like "I'm more motivated than ever", or "Alyssa would like me better if I weighed less", or "I really enjoy vegetables", or "Mom understands and is trying to cook low fat meals", and much more. All the good things. The list under "Negative forces" might include "I'm practically addicted to Pizza", "I'm famished when I get home from school", or "We all stop for ice cream on the way home from school" or "I eat too much just before I go to bed"

When you have as many items as your child can think of, turn each one of these forces into an action statement. Given where I am, where I want to get, and the forces that are keeping me at the current situation, how can I increase the number or strength of the positive forces, and decrease the number and strength of the negative forces? What is implied by "I eat too much just before I go to bed"? These can then be turned into an action plan. It might be the simple listing of what I will try to do, or it could be more complex with dates , sub steps, and more.

The example here with weight control is for illustrative purposes. The important Learn to Learn issue is that your child can learn a system for making more reasoned and deliberate decisions in his life, rather that being subject too heavily to peer pressure, or using a whim of the moment. Starting small can develop these Learn to Learn skills so that when the big decisions come along, your child will be better prepared.

Again, the best parental role is supporting the child's own learning processes rather than giving direct advice. There is clearly room for direct advice, even absolute prohibitions or requirements ("No, you may not ride your bicycle across the freeway!") But seriously, as much as possible, help your child to be responsible herself. Respect <u>her</u> judgment.

With respect to this issue, here is what <u>I</u> can do to help <u>my</u> child:

17. Involvement in Planning Learning

I'm always more interested in learning if I have been a part of the planning, and I'm sure this is true of almost everyone. If the course is designed with my needs in mind, if I am asked what the emphasis should be, I am much more motivated than if the curriculum is designed by someone else, meant to fit everyone's needs and interests. If what an instructor planned seemed dull, or something I already knew pretty well, or didn't think I needed to know, I would ask the teacher if I could do something different. Not whining, or fussing and complaining, but saying that I thought I would learn more if I did a project instead of a paper, or did some interviews in the community about a topic, or write a journal, or whatever. Many times the teacher was willing, and in addition to my being more motivated, I was letting the teacher know that I was interested in the class, and trying to learn a lot. Teachers appreciate that.

But I am speaking of higher education. As a university teacher I could ask the students what direction they wanted to take, give them choices between, say, a paper or a journal, drop or add topics depending on the skills and the needs of the students.

This concept is much more difficult in elementary, middle and high schools. Schools and teachers have determined what children need to know, and essentially they are right, at least for most kids, and most of the time. Further, teachers have an enormously difficult task, usually with a large group. It's difficult to impossible to really individualize the content. But there is still much that can be done; a considerable degree of latitude that the teacher and the child can utilize. Parents can help here too.

You can encourage your child to take advantage of any choices the teacher is able to offer. Some times a choice is available between, for example, which historical figure to study in more depth, or which current events topic to write about. Help the child be aware of the choices, and make a selection that he will find relevant and even exciting.

Or a child can ask for more latitude. "May I read about the Lewis and Clark expedition instead of the conquistadors? We are planning a family vacation next summer near where they traveled. I could look it up on the internet and write a report, too".

Or "My Grandpa was my age when the second World War started. Could I interview him and report to the class about what it was like to be a young boy then?"

And without pandering to the teacher, he could genuinely ask for some help in how to go about an assignment, given a special interest.

With respect to this issue, here is what I can do to help my child:

18. Using the EAT Model

Here's a teaching technique that I use with university students, which I offer only as an example. It is illustrative of a very important point I want to make, one that is at the heart of the ideas in this booklet. Please think of how you can adapt this model to your own relationship with your child.

I teach a course in management in which teamwork is one topic. The traditional way to teach this unit, consistent with the "I know-you-don't-I'm-going-to-tell-you" style of teaching is to ask the students to read the chapter in the text about teamwork, give a lecture and lead a discussion about teamwork, and maybe have the students write a paper about teamwork. The point, of course, is to have them learn <u>about</u> teamwork.

I have a somewhat different goal, and a different approach. Understand, there is nothing wrong with the transfer model of learning, learning <u>about</u> things, but that it is not enough. My students indeed need to know more about teamwork, but they also need to be better team members and team leaders, that is, to have additional <u>skill</u>, not just knowledge. And knowledge and skill are two different things.

I use a technique called "The Non-verbal Puzzle" to help my MBA students learn to be better team members. Groups of five students stand at a table, and are given packets of puzzle pieces, with the instruction that each person on the team is to have a completed 6" square puzzle in front of him. I assign a student observer to each group. The pieces in the packets are arranged so that cooperation is required. Students share pieces, working on their own puzzle but also being aware of the puzzles of the others in their group, or team. The 20 minutes or so required for the five individuals in each group to complete their puzzles demonstrates a wide variety of teamwork skills. The groups that use the most effective teamwork skills are the ones that complete the puzzle most quickly.

After each group has completed its puzzles, I have the observers report on what they had noticed when the groups were working. For example, it is possible to complete an individual puzzle using the wrong pieces, so that others on the team cannot complete theirs. Sometimes a member of a team is so possessive about his own completed puzzle that he is unwilling to break it up for the benefit of the entire team. Students analyze their performance in detail. I list the elements of teamwork that they noticed (on the board) and lead a discussion.

I then ask the puzzle teams to meet again, with the observer, to discuss the implications of the list, and their skill in doing the puzzle. What generalizations can be drawn? Given their experience, what theme can be inclusive of the elements we discussed? Then we determine and discuss the generalizations that can be drawn from the experience. "What sort of a theory of teamwork could you develop", I ask the class.

This pattern, sometimes called experiential learning, is readily translatable to the world of children, and is the basic theme of this booklet.

I use a key word to describe it and have tried to focus my own teaching and parenting as much as possible in this direction, providing experiential learning patterns. Let's also call it learning to learn. That is, once learned, it can be applied to the next learning situation and the next, and the next. It is at the heart of lifelong learning.

The key word is E A T. Easy enough to remember. The letters stand for <u>E</u>xperience, <u>A</u>nalysis, and <u>T</u>heory.

In the traditional model, "I-know-you-don't-I'm-going-to-tell-you", the pattern starts with the T or <u>Theory</u>. For children this might be the "big idea" and the teacher simply explains it, or it could even be merely a vocabulary list. Next the big idea, or Theory, is <u>Analyzed</u>. The teacher explains what the big idea means, what the parts and pieces of it are. Then comes the Experience, or application. Sometimes this is a real application, such as the children doing something to illustrate the concept, or a laboratory session in a physics class. Sometimes it is a further presentation by the teacher, telling about the application.

With experiential education, or in the Learn to Learn mode, the order is reversed. This is the pattern I suggest you use when helping your child.

Please understand that the pattern must be adjusted to match the developmental stage of the child. If your child is in the third grade, the content is one thing; if a senior in high school, the content is obviously quite different. But the pattern is identical!

Start with an experience or a discussion of the experience. It might be a simple question about a school activity or an outside of school experience. Get as much information from your child as is comfortable for him. (Teenagers are tough!).

Then lead the child to analyze the experience. "What are the parts of it?"; "How does this connect with things you have done before, or know about from another source?"; What do you think about this?"; and even "How did doing it (the experience the child described) make you feel?"

The third step is the most difficult, especially with a young child. It is an attempt to have the child generalize from the experience and the analysis of it. "What does it all mean? "How would you describe the whole thing? What principles can you figure out from all of it?" "What will you know next time you work with this issue?"

Try to remember E A T and use it as a mechanism to help your child understand his school experiences. It can make an enormous difference in his life!

With respect to this issue, here is what I can do to help my child:

19. Case Studies

Case studies are often used in college courses, especially in the social sciences and in management, to come as close as possible to providing a "real" experience for students. They are equally applicable in children's learning, and are an excellent example of a Learn to Learn technique. Further, they can readily be used by parents, and generally are fun for children. Many children's books are written as case studies, as are cartoon sequences, computer characters, and kids' TV programs

As a parent, you might simply set the stage by asking your child to pretend to be, for example, an historic figure. "The country is in a serious depression, most people are out of work, many are hungry,...." "What would you do if you were President Roosevelt?" Then help your child to understand the moves that Roosevelt made to try to solve those problems.

Cases can be done easily in a simple conversational setting, and are even amenable to helping a child with a personal problem, such as how to deal with a bully on the playground, or understanding how to improve relationships with a friend or with a teacher; or for ethical dilemmas, such as whether or not to report someone who is cheating.

Or you and your child might <u>write</u> a case, perhaps based on a real situation in the child's life that needs attention, with details about the situation, then ask the child to analyze the case and solve the problem. "What would you do if...?"

The move from an <u>Experience</u>, even a virtual experience like a case, to an <u>Analysis</u> of the experience, to the generation of an encompassing <u>Theory</u> is illustrative of a learning process that can be applied again and again. It's important though, that the "processing" be deliberate and complete. In language appropriate to your child's age, ask "What problem solving techniques did you use?"; "How did you move from the problem to a solution?" "How could you go through this system of problem solving even better next time?" All these are questions that can help the child to focus on the "how" of his learning.

With respect to this issue, here is what <u>I</u> can do to help <u>my</u> child:

20. Role Play; Role Reversal

Using role pay is another kind of "simulation" which can be fun and very illustrative of the processes of learning. It avoids putting the child in the role of sponge, soaking up the knowledge being dispensed by his elders, and provides a more active scenario. Taking a role is non-threatening, but provides a setting around which many learning processes can be woven. It also helps a child Learn to Learn from other cultures, religions and nationalities. If your child thinks that the teacher is too demanding, or doesn't like your child, or...., you might set up a role play in which your child takes the teacher role and you the child's. Have a conversation, but be sure to stick with the roles. After you work with it for a few minutes, help the child to analyze the role play, then come to conclusions. Avoid the temptation to provide the conclusions yourself, however.

If the topic is one in which there are two distinct sides, a role play can be extremely effective. If, for example, the issue in a high school class in current events is the Palestine-Israel conflict, one of you could take the role of the Israeli, the other the role of the Palestinian, and have a conversation. For a useful twist, after you have each expressed the position of your role, reverse the roles, and argue for the other side. Again, take the time to consider, with the child, how it went and what you each learned from the role play, not only about the Palestine-Israel issue but also how to profitably discuss an issue, and how to learn from it.

With respect to this issue, here is what I can do to help my child:

21. Teamwork

In sports, in the modern corporation or small business, and finally in schools, there has been increased recognition that tasks are often best accomplished by groups of people functioning as a team. Schools are increasingly recognizing that teamwork skills are quite learnable, and thus teachable. Some enlightened schools are providing grades for the ability to work with others. Learning is not always a solitary occupation.

There are skills associated with teamwork which you can identify and reinforce. Leadership is the obvious example, but only an involving rather than bossy kind of leadership. Encourage your child to take part in team activities, be as cooperative as possible rather than competitive, be able to submerge his own ego at times to benefit the group. In a basketball game this often means passing off to a teammate who probably has a better chance of scoring than you. The teammate gets the credit for the shot, but the passer gets an assist, and the team gets the points. Let's help kids learn that the assists are often just as important as the score.

You might encourage your child to have friends over to the house to work on class projects, or to plan and complete an activity associated with a club or organization, like your church, or the Boy Scouts. Working well together is an important Learn to Learn task, an strangely enough, two plus two can equal five!

With respect to this issue, here is what I can do to help my child:

22. Learn to Learn and Gender

A substantial amount of research has been accomplished in recent years, as part of the gender equity focus, to evaluate gender differences in learning. Much of the earlier research on learning was done on boys, and the results are not always applicable to girls. Girls are less inclined than boys, for example, to get involved in class discussions, to raise their hand to ask questions, or to offer comments. Some studies have also indicated that teachers are more responsive to boys, more inclined to call on them, more supportive of their activities in class. If your child is a girl, you might think about these generalizations and see if they apply in her case. If so, try to encourage more involvement on her part in class. Try to reinforce positively her descriptions of her own contributions and help her to feel more confident about taking part.

Girls often are credited very properly with a greater intuitive sense than boys and greater comfort in learning through feelings. Your questions about how she feels about issues in school might strengthen and support this aspect of her learning style.

There are enormous implications for girls in a wonderful book, "Women's Ways of Knowing, by Belenky, et al. It is a detailed study of how women learn and know. One important concept is the change from a child as a sponge, not taking part, all the learning flying above her, to a second stage, the absolute trust of an authority, like a teacher or a book. But the third, representing full maturity of learning, is the ability to be one's own learner, to put things together, to integrate experiences into a personally developed construct. I'm sure this also applies to males, but it is a fascinating look at how our culture treats female children.

With respect to this issue, here is what I can do to help my child:

23. Research methods

I remember learning a lot about learning, or at least the answer to the question "How do I know that?', by taking several courses in research methods: how to design experiments and how to use statistics. What does correlation mean? How should I react to TV ads claiming great powers for a medication? How can I be skeptical without being cynical? What does it mean when cause and effect is implied, but only a relationship is indicated? Surely there are ways to learn these problem-solving and learning issues at the level of the elementary school as well as graduate school.

One of the most important ways of getting new information - by new I mean previously unknown by anyone - is to conduct research. In a small way, we all conduct research all the time. We can help our kids to be "researchers"; helping them to learn the steps and systems that scientists use to move beyond the edge of that which is already known.

A few memories - When I was about 7 years old, I remember a conversation with my parents. They were interested in saving water. My mother was upset at the size of the water bill. The conversation turned to the question of whether a bath or shower used more water. My dad thought a shower took less, and my mother's guess was a tub. I had no idea, but somehow came up with a way to tell. I suggested that the next time someone took a shower they could close the drain, and at the end of the shower, see how much water it used compared to a bath. I thought at the time that it was a brilliant stroke, and strangely, I still remember it. I suppose it's possible that my parents led me to the idea somehow, but then again, maybe I thought of it all by myself. I surely remember the thrill I had about coming up with such a great experiment!

Years later, when teaching an eighth grade science class, a question arose about how to ripen green tomatoes, picked to avoid a frost. Several students thought that they should be left on the counter in the kitchen, and they would ripen after a few days. Several others thought that they should be covered with a dish, because they had read an ad for a dish made for the purpose. Some said that putting them in a paper bag was the thing to do, because that's what their grandmother always did. I just plain didn't know. I asked them how we could find out for sure.

So the students devised a research study. They brought in a bunch of green tomatoes, we randomized them as much as possible according to size, greenness/redness, variety and I suppose other factors, then made up three groups of a dozen or so each. One group we left uncovered, one group we put under a glass bowl, and one group in a paper bag. We put them in equivalent places, and waited to see what would happen.

Sorry- I can't remember the results about the tomatoes, but I do remember the fun the students had in conducting research, randomizing, developing a scale to evaluate the ripeness, and taking part in the associated discussions.

We dealt fully with the question, asked quite seriously, "How do you know that?" Maybe the claims of a company that sells glass covers for ripening tomatoes are not totally accurate. Maybe family lore handed down for generations is not accurate either!

The next time your child has a question and you honestly don't know the answer, try the response "I really don't know. How can we find out?", and see if your child can get a research study underway.

With respect to this issue, here is what I can do to help my child:

24. Questionnaires

A popular teaching technique in graduate schools is the use of instruments. A questionnaire about one's managerial role, for example, can be scored into a pattern so that the student gets a view, however accurate, about his/her managerial style. One I used frequently in a course called "Human Relations in Business and Industry" is called FIRO-B. It is based on a model of social psychology, and gives scores for several issues in interpersonal relations, such as control. One gets a score for the extent to which he/she is comfortable directing others, as well as being directed by others. After the experience of taking and scoring the instrument, I would have students analyze the results in small groups, then come to generalizations. Much more fun, more experiential, more motivational and more useful than the traditional lecture about the issue of control in relationships at work.

Instruments can be used very successfully by parents of school age children. Often they can be found in magazines, as some sort of "personality inventory", or "Test your baseball IQ", or "What is your physical fitness index?", and many more. Instruments are often found on the internet. These can readily form the "experience" portion of the "Experience - Analysis - Theory" pattern, described in No. 18. Ask your child to take the instrument, and, if appropriate, take it yourself. After scoring it, help the child to analyze the results, and discuss the results as compared with your own. You might even ask your child for suggestions about how you might behave differently as a result of your scores, assuming you agree that the scores really reflect your situation. The pattern of converting an experience to more generalized learning can intuitively be translated to other learning situations. It is a way to learn which has very wide applicability.

With respect to this issue, here is what I can do to help my child:

25. Support Your Child's Projects

Projects, such as science projects, are fortunately a favorite technique of many enlightened teachers. Children can be helped to determine for themselves an interesting topic or a question that they would like to answer. Projects are highly motivational, for this very reason, and are another excellent way to use the model E -A -T . Sometimes in schools, however, projects turn into an opportunity for merely showcasing the students' work, and the Learn to Learn aspects are lost.

One way you can help is by being responsible for the "processing" of the project into real learning. Ask your child details about the school project, trying to elicit the child's thoughts and feelings about how he learned from doing the project, not only what he learned. One of the primary limitations of even competent teachers, especially in this time of increasing reliance on achievement test scores, is the failure to do this processing adequately, which means that many Learn-to-Learn opportunities are missed.

You can also undertake projects of your own with your child. What a wonderful way to become a colleague of your youngster as you work together on an issue which you both want to explore. The project might involve the use of reference materials, interviews with persons in the community who have useful information, the use of the astounding research capabilities of the internet, and many other activities the two of you can undertake as colleagues in the learning process. Again, the important part might well be not so much the experience of the research, or the interview, or the other learning activities, but rather the careful and complete move from the experience to an analysis of it, to the generalizations. Make sure that the process is quite deliberate, and that your child understands the steps, so that it becomes an internalized tool of learning as he/she builds a repertoire of Learn to Learn techniques.

With respect to this issue, here is what I can do to help my child:

26. Field Trips

How about using a family trip or even a vacation as the source of learning for your child? "Of course," you say. "Easy. I do it all the time." But I'm suggesting that in addition to the usual, like pointing out scenic sights, mentioning local history, visiting museums, checking out maps, and all the other great opportunities for learning while on a trip, that you also consider the learning to learn implications. If your child points out that it's almost 200 miles from home to Denver, be sure to focus on how the child knew that, and reward the process of learning as well as having the information. Be sure to help your child sharpen his observational skills by reinforcing his ability to notice things along the way. You might have him help you plan the trip, or be the navigator. After the museum or a stop at the visitor center, discuss yourself what you learned or saw, and how it connects with what you already knew. Be sure to let your youngster know that you find pleasure in learning new things and in putting the new ideas together with older information. Speculate. "I wonder what this stretch of highway looked like 100 years ago". Let the child know that you honor his questions, by answering carefully, after letting him know that it was a good question, and why. "I wonder what kind of bird that is? Let's look it up in the guide when we get home!" Again, your own attitude makes an enormous difference.

A related idea is to plan a visit to a museum or similar place specifically for learning how to learn. You could explain where you are going, what is there, and ask the child what he might expect to find there, and what he will look for. And on the way home, discuss what he did see, and how it compared with his expectations. "What surprised you the most? "What was the most interesting thing you learned?"

You might suggest that your child keep a journal, perhaps including drawings of things he sees along the way, or use the family camera or a camera of his own.

It's relatively easy to do, and helps children to learn from their own experience rather than merely from presentations or a book. It also helps to define the parental role as one who arranging resources rather than simply being the expert; more of a colleague of the child's, less the boss.

With respect to this issue, here is what I can do to help my child:

27. Study Skills

One aspect of learning to learn, if a bit on the mundane side, is the area of study skills and memory aids. These are often taught in schools and can be very useful. Here are a few from my memory and my experience as a student.

SQ3R

I don't remember where I first encountered this, but it is a reading skill that has made a substantial difference in my life, I'm sure. Bless the teacher who shared it with me! It's merely a pattern for effective reading of nonfiction that helps one to get maximum information from reading.

• The "S" stands for Survey, and for me this means scanning the table of contents and looking at how the chapters are organized. Are there any exercises or other useful supplements at the end of each chapter, is there a bibliography, or other similar aids. I read the information on the jacket and the preface, look over photos, charts and tables, and in general get an idea of what this book or article is going to be about.

• "Q" means question. I ask myself what I will learn from this book, what questions will it answer for me, how will it fit into my existing frames of reference, how will it relate to what I already know?

• The first R is for Read. I read the book, sometimes almost skimming if the information is not relevant to me, or I know it already; sometimes very carefully, repeating sentences and paragraphs if necessary. I underline, write in the margins, and use a highlighter. I keep my questions from the "Q" stage in mind.

• The second R is for Review. I go back over any especially interesting or useful parts, paying close attention to my marginal notes and highlighting. I pay particular attention to how the various pieces of the book relate to each other, and try to formulate connections, summarize concepts, make generalizations. Were my questions answered?

• The final R stands for Recite. Not necessarily in the traditional way, but I try to find someone to tell about what I have learned. (Emma, our Welsh Corgi, listens very well, and cocks her head to let me know if an idea appeals to her.) Sometimes my reciting takes the form of a few minutes spent at the word processor writing notes about the book or article.

This is merely one of many study skills. Even the youngest child can use it, or an adaptation of it.

And although study skills generally have to do with a relatively simple kind of learning, almost rote, they can be crucial, and make the difference between success and failure in school. Other more general study skills include how to use a library, using the internet, how to read charts and tables, and many more.

Mnemonic (great word, isn't it?) devices are simple little systems for remembering things. Two come to mind. One is the little ditty "Every good boy deserves friends". My 7th grade music teacher, Mrs. Pearl Gage Allen (I wonder why I remember her full name?) taught us this to remember the notes in the scale; E,G,B,D,F. It is now many years later, and I still have it. Another is "On old Olympus' towering top, a Finn and German vined some hops". This is a clue to the first letters of the names of the cranial nerves, which I needed to know for a course in anatomy. Olfactory, oculomotor, optic, trigeminal,.... I'll quit while I'm ahead. Again, the kind of learning supported here is simple- just rote memory- but (perhaps unfortunately) useful for passing tests. I even seem to remember making up my own poems or sayings to remember other lists of points for tests.

With respect to this issue, here is what I̲ can do to help m̲y̲ child:

28. Learning to Learn Citizenship

When my parents went to school they studied "Civics". In my day, it was "Problems of Democracy". Now there seems to be very little of the curriculum devoted to the idea of becoming an effective citizen, but the concept is even more important than it was. However, since Civics and Problems of Democracy were strongly on the side of indoctrination, even indoctrination into the values we all consider important - democracy, liberty - maybe we can do even better with a Learn to Learn approach to teaching citizenship. It is certainly crucial, especially in a democracy, that the electorate be informed. Democracy could not function without independent thought. And yet we are besieged on every side with the admonition to follow the party line, to do what we are told, to agree with the leadership. Lately, if one does not agree, one even runs the risk of being branded as unpatriotic. I recently wanted to find out for myself what the cultural mores and political views of the residents of Middle America were. What and how do people think about current issues? I took a cross country motorcycle trip, partly to learn what I could about the attitudes and values of people whose political views were probably very different than my own. It was just before the beginning of the Iraq invasion. I stopped for breakfast at a cafe in a very small town. The only person there, a cheerful and charming lady, was the owner, the cook, and the waitress. I was the only customer. I asked her, "What do you suppose most people around here think about our invading Iraq?". She didn't know what I meant. As best I could tell, she didn't know that

Iraq was a country. She said "All people talk about around here is whether or not it's going to rain".

Do all that you can to help your child to become an active and thoughtful citizen of local government, state and national government, and indeed a citizen of the entire planet.

A few specific activities:

• Make sure that your child is aware of your own civic concerns; not only your support of a political party, but your reasons.

• When there are neighborhood activities, fund drives, meetings to decide positions on road improvements or bond issues, be sure that your youngster is involved along with you. Take your child with you to vote. Be sure that he sees it as a real honor to be able to vote, to express one's opinion, and how each vote counts. Make sure he knows that you have been very thoughtful about deciding who and what to vote for.

• Discuss the news daily with your child, from TV, newspapers or magazines. "I see in the paper that the city council is to vote on a bond issue for road improvement. Do you have an opinion on that? How would you vote if you were a council member?"

• This is a great opportunity for role play with your child, which can be a lot of fun. Each of you take the role of a candidate, or a position on a civic issue, including national concerns like pollution control, environmental concerns, or immigration issues. Listen carefully to his position, and help him to understand yours without being overbearing.

With respect to this issue, here is what I can do to help my child:

29. Dealing With "One Size Fits All" Education

Recent work by Howard Gardner about multiple intelligence is on the Learning to Learn side of the ledger. Gardner points out that there is much more to intelligence than the cognitive, the form of intelligence which is measured by intelligence tests. He describes other aspects of intelligence, such as spatial, bodily-kinesthetic, interpersonal and intrapersonal, even musical - which are rarely given their full due by teachers.

Some experts suggest that we emphasize using the learning style that the child has problems with, to develop that strength. Some, however, feel that it makes more sense to bypass the problem, and simply learn with another modality. If that is the case, as it seems best to me, the parental role might well be to help the child find another way to learn if the traditional one is a problem. In any case, your focus should be on understanding a difficulty and supporting the child's efforts.

A wonderful book is available ("A Mind at a Time" by Mel Levine, M.D.) written by a pioneer in helping us all to understand that a "one-size-fits-all" education, unfortunately a system that busy and pressured schools often adopt, can cause children to struggle because their learning patterns don't fit the requirements of their schools. The author is a pediatrician who has studied children's learning patterns. From the book jacket...

"In 'A Mind at a Time', Dr. Levine shows parents and others who care for children how to identify these individual learning patterns. He explains how parents and teachers can encourage a child's strengths and bypass the child's weaknesses. This type of teaching provides satisfaction and achievement instead of frustration and failure."

"Different brains are differently wired, Dr. Levine explains. There are eight fundamental systems, or components, of learning, that draw on a variety of neurodevelopment capacities. Some students are strong in certain areas and some are strong in others, but no one is equally capable in all eight. Using examples drawn from his own extensive experience, Dr. Levine

shows how parents and children can identify their strengths and weaknesses to determine their individual learning styles".

"For example, some students are creative and write imaginatively, but do poorly in history because weak memory skills prevent them from retaining facts. Some students are weak in sequential ordering and can't follow directions. They may test poorly and often don't do well in mathematics. In these cases, Dr. Levine observes, the problem is not a lack of intelligence, but a learning style that doesn't fit the assignment. Drawing on his pioneering research and his work with thousands of students, Dr. Levine shows how parents and teachers can develop effective strategies to work through or around these weaknesses".

The book provides wonderful insights for parents and teachers. Most chapters conclude with a section entitled "Practical Considerations."

Help your child to focus on his learning skills, to learn about his own learning styles and preferences, and evaluate and improve them.

With respect to this issue, here is what I can do to help my child:

30. Be Your Own Teacher

Years ago, John Dewey, the great educational philosopher who initiated the "progressive" school of thought,
said that a truly educated person is one who has become
his/her own teacher. If we were really competent at learn-
ing- at the processes of learning - we would be our own
teacher. Not as an expert, but as one who knows how to
get the answers. Think about how to help your child to
become his/her own teacher. What is it that a teacher does
that really works? How does a teacher lead a child to discovery? How can the child do it himself?

I have always found that I really learned something
best when I tried to teach it to someone else. I had to think
about how to organize the information and present it, how
to be clear, how to understand the issues from the perspective of the learner.

Kids love to play school, and this should certainly be
encouraged. If your child plays school with other kids,
you could reinforce the activity.

But by far the most important activity is to genuinely ask your child to teach you. What a thrill for a child to be able to teach an adult, especially a parent! You need to be honest, not condescending. And again, the child will learn the material best by teaching it to you.

With respect to this issue, here is what I can do to help my child:

31. Writing a Journal

Just like a "project", writing a journal can be an excellent way to help your child Learn to Learn, and at the same time a delightful way to communicate with your child as a colleague rather than a boss. Many children love to keep a diary. With appropriate reinforcement and care that the child's privacy is not infringed upon, the diary or journal serves as a personal sounding board for the child's own learning processes. You might start by suggesting the child write a simple description of what he did today, or this week, then ask him to tell you about it or read it to you. Be an appreciative audience, and help with the processing of the experiences. "That must have been interesting/difficult/important for you. What did you learn from doing that"? You also might help by suggesting questions to which your child could respond in the journal, such as "I was attracted to doing this because…", "Here's what I did", "Here's how it felt to do that", "Here's how I'm going to do it differently next time", and "Here's what I learned from doing it". The journal can include sketches or collages or song lyrics or quotations, or whatever. It's perfectly OK if the entries are cryptic and include spelling or grammatical errors. Skillful technical use of language will come as time goes on; a journal should just be a way to express oneself and have fun, especially with you as your child's colleague.

With respect to this issue, here is what I can do to help my child:

32. Cause and Effect

One measure of maturity and very much related to the skill of being one's own learner, is an understanding of cause and effect. "When I do ....., the result is.... But when I do .... instead, then ...happens". Our lessons from experience teach us quickly not to touch a hot stove, and to have a drink when we are thirsty. But some more subtle experiences need a bit of explanation for a child to connect cause with effect. The parent is the ideal source of feedback here.

Unfortunately, many parents turn this feedback into negative evaluation, even including a subtle or not so subtle "I told you so!", as in "I told you if you didn't study more you'd screw up that math test". Try to make sure that you never use an empty threat, like "If you don't do your homework right now, you can't go with us to the park", then relent and take the child to the park. If you do make such a threat, probably not a good idea in the first place, make sure that the consequence you described really happens. It takes only a few lessons for the child when the threat is not followed up, to realize that the threat didn't mean much; cause does not connect with effect. Try instead to model the cause and effect thinking with your child; think out loud with your child. You might recall for the child previous experiences of a similar nature, and remind him what happened that time.

The point is, don't get between the cause and effect for your child. Allow the natural consequences, short of safety, or creating a problem, of course, to be the result. It's probably more functional to point out the happy consequences than the painful ones. We all need to learn that our behaviors have consequences; this is the heart of the Learn to Learn process. A classic seems to me to be the parent who wants the child to come along, the child lags behind, the parent says "Bye-bye" as she heads to the car in the parking lot. Surely the child either is frightened, or knows full well that this is an empty threat, and thus a lie. Neither is functional.

With respect to this issue, here is what I can do to help my child:

33. Puzzles

Puzzles of all sorts can be very useful ways to learn patterns, logical thinking, a systems approach, and problem solving in general. Simple crossword puzzles, aimed at your child's age level, can be fun and very rewarding. Again, the question "How did you know how to do that?" can be very useful in helping a child to become his own teacher, to learn the processes of learning. Some textbooks have simulations of one kind or another included in the textbook or at the end of chapters. Children's books are usually loaded with interesting puzzles. Newspapers and magazines have puzzles; mystery books are essentially puzzles requiring logic for determining the solution. The important part is to do whatever you can to help the child to discover how his own brain and feelings best work to provide him with solutions to problems. Completing a puzzle or solving a mystery is just the first step. Most of the learning comes from a very deliberate consideration of the techniques the child used in order to complete it. Moving from the experience to an analysis of the experience to the development of generalizations is not automatic, any more than learning mathematics automatically teaches one how to think. It needs support, and is the ideal role for the parent/colleague.

With respect to this issue, here is what I can do to help my child:

34. From the Philosophers

The idea of learning to learn, or process learning, is certainly not new. Many people over the years have written about it in one form or another, and it rests on sound educational philosophy. Should you want to pursue the topic in a more philosophical setting, you might take a look at a book about the work of John Dewey, probably America's greatest educational philosopher and intellectual father of the "progressive" school of education. It's called "What Every Great Teacher Knows: Practical Principles for Effective Teaching". The authors are Richard Gibboney and Clark Webb. The publisher is Holistic Education Press, Brandon, VT. Holistic Press, incidentally, has published many very interesting and useful books about learning and teaching. Their web site is at www.great-ideas.org. This one is a very practical distillation of Dewey's work into eighteen major principles, each of which can readily be translated into practical steps for a parent. Despite the title, it is as useful for parents as for teachers. One of Dewey's great ideas is that a truly educated person is one who no longer needs a teacher; that is, is a self- learner.

The other philosopher who dealt primarily with process learning is Alfred North Whitehead. The definitive essay he wrote is "The Aims of Education". It is contained in a book of his writings, "The Aims of Education and Other Essays", published by The Free Press, New York, I won't try to explain Whitehead's positions, but a pattern he proposed is similar to my Experience-Analysis-Theory sequence. His words are Romance- Precision - Generalization. I find his writing a bit opaque, but his ideas are fantastic.

Another, more accessible work about Whitehead is Malcolm D. Evan's book, "Whitehead and Philosophy of Education", published by Rodopi, of Atlanta and Amsterdam.

All three are available through Amazon.com

With respect to this issue, here is what I can do to help my child:

35. How to Relate to Peers

If your child is an adolescent or even preadolescent, you are aware of the importance of peer culture. Kids of this age find it of crucial importance to fit in with others, to be "part of the gang". Rather than seeing this as a threat, you might associate it with the Learn to Learn idea, and use the peer culture to your child's advantage. Be sure to encourage connections between your child and other kids, especially those who seem to like school and are interested in learning, even for the sake of learning. Try to be as interested in the friend's schoolwork as you are in your own child's. Encourage your own youngster to learn from his friends and to teach his friends, to form alliances, to share ideas about homework or exciting ways to solve problems. When you take your own child on a field trip, a visit to a museum, or a tour of a business, ask your child if he would like to invite a friend or two. Encourage them to figure things out, and reward the process. Help them to talk about school and how they have learned what they know.

If your child is younger, you are aware how little kids, even preschoolers, love to "play school". Some reinforcement here can work wonders in establishing positive attitudes toward the entire school experience, the joy of learning, and functional relationships with other children.

With respect to this issue, here is what I can do to help my child:

36. Formation of Values

Values which come from outside ourselves - parents, church, teachers, and the moral values of a culture, form our initial morality and determine our initial behaviors. These behaviors, however, can lead to consequences and feedback which conflict with those values as well as support them. The child, therefore, properly moves into his own cycle of behaving, experiencing the consequences, and readjusting his values. Only when this happens are the values personally appropriated and therefore useful in determining behavior. It's much different for a child to refrain from cheating because his mother says it's bad, and refraining from cheating because he personally believes that cheating is wrong; that it conflicts with his own values.

The Learn to Learn framework can help you help your child to become a values oriented person. You must, of course, model moral behavior yourself, and don't hesitate to explain to your child what values are acceptable, and expected. If you are honest, expect your child to be honest. If you believe that violence solves problems, expect your child to believe that violence solves problems. But go beyond modeling to help your child discover for himself the happy results of, say, honesty. The Learn to Learn child is thus in the process of developing a personal ethical system, a method for evaluating and reevaluating his own behaviors and therefore has the comfort of a functional, living code.

You and your child might have fun working on simple moral dilemmas. "What would you do if..." You can provide the context, appropriate to the child's age and interests. Your position is not to determine the right responses, but rather help your child to discover appropriate responses. Ethical maturity goes from the simplest - decisions based on what feels good or doesn't hurt - to following the law or the rules and regulations, to a much more complex system, based more on one's conscience. If your moral dilemma is something like "What would you do if you saw another kid in school cheating?", one answer might be to tell the teacher. But that might be neither the most ethical response, nor the response that would lead to a more ethical classroom. Talking over values-oriented issues with your youngster can go a long way toward helping your child Learn to Learn about valuing, and to develop an ethical system.

With respect to this issue, here is what I can do to help my child:

37. A Sense of Responsibility

Learning to Learn is a classic example of a personal sense of responsibility.

L2L means moving away from the assumption that the teacher or parent has the responsibility for the child's learning, and recognition that basic responsibility centers on the child. There are many ways for a parent to induce a strong sense of responsibility in a child.

The first is, once again, the idea of modeling. If you as a parent are willing to accept responsibility for your own missteps and take the blame, as well as assuming the rewards for your own good decisions, your child will pick up on this and more readily see cause and effect in his own life. It doesn't have to be evaluative and associated with reward and punishment, but rather a straightforward recognition of causes and results.

When your child does a good job, be sure that you point out to him that the pleasant effects came as a result of sensible decisions on his part and were not a matter of luck. Be careful that you don't overdo it, though. Just a kind of natural, "You planned that carefully and studied thoroughly, so as you can see, the results are excellent. You really have amazing skill as the result of your careful preparation."

Be sure you don't get in the way of the sequence of results. Threats are never useful, I suspect, but if you are moved to say something like "If you do ......, I'll have to ...." be sure that it's realistic in the first place, not said in anger. And be sure to follow through. If the consequences are as described, you won't have to say "I told you so...", but the child will quickly realize himself that all behaviors have consequences, and that wise decisions make for desirable consequences. Be especially careful to point out the rewards that come with good decisions. "You did a great job with that, and it's probably because you listened carefully to the teacher. Good for you !" "You learned that really well; you must be very proud of yourself".

With respect to this issue, here is what I can do to help my child:

38. Flexibility or Fundamentalism?

Flexibility is an important virtue in today's sometimes chaotic world. The ability to see both sides of an argument, to assess ones' own understandings and be able to make appropriate changes as situations change and more information becomes available is a characteristic of someone engaged in the process of learning; someone who is a learner, not merely learned. Being comfortable with change is crucial to a fulfilling life in today's rapidly changing world.

Flexibility and learning to learn are consistent with democracy; fundamentalism and indoctrination are more consistent with autocracy.

Tolerance for ambiguity, a related theme, is equally important. Flexibility and tolerance for ambiguity are the direct opposite of fundamentalism. And fundamentalism - hanging on to an idea or value without adequate evaluation - is obviously counterproductive to learning. Fundamentalists rigidly stick with a position even in the face of conflicting evidence. They are not inclined to figure things out, to solve problems. They already have the answers. In your connections with your child, remember that it's perfectly OK to be tentative, to be other than an expert. It's even completely OK not to know something. A very adequate response to a child's question is "Hmm; that's a good question and I sure don't know the answer. How can we find out?" Don't be afraid to be tentative, even unsure. Emphasize and model for your child your own processes of seeking answers rather than merely <u>having</u> the answers. A sentence beginning with "On the other hand..." can be very useful. Tentativeness also allows room for the child's thinking and searching for the answer. Swallow your ego and your need to be the expert; join with your child in the search. Be flexible and even tentative rather than a fundamentalist. The world is not black and white, and that's perfectly OK. There are lots of things you don't know, and that's OK too. Questions are more useful than answers. You will be a better model for your child as a learn<u>er</u>, than as learn<u>ed</u>!

With respect to this issue, here is what <u>I</u> can do to help <u>my</u> child:

39. Listening

Probably the greatest gift you can give your child is to be a good listener. Listening is a complex skill, something we do not only with our ears, but with all of us. And listening rates with reading in its importance as a process skill in learning to learn. Being a good listener is probably even more difficult than becoming a good reader. Fortunately, the schools are emphasizing listening skills much more today than even a few years ago.

Here are a few specific suggestions for helping your child to be a better listener.

• Listen carefully and enthusiastically yourself, especially to your child. This doesn't mean being quiet. A good listener asks questions, seeks clarification, comments briefly, but keeps the focus of the communication on the speaker.

• Draw out the child, be appreciative, tell him what your thoughts and feelings are with respect to what he is saying. And be patient. Learning to listen is a very difficult task for a child, especially an ebullient, effervescent youngster who need to express himself a lot.

• Be sure to reinforce good listening skills on the part of your child. A simple "You are a really good listener!" will be of enormous use in helping your child to focus on listening skills.

• You might check out the International Listening Association web site at www.listen.org to get some ideas. They have fun exercises you might be able to try with your child. But remember, it's the two of you learning together, not merely you "teaching" your child.

With respect to this issue, here is what I can do to help my child:

40. Competition/Cooperation

Many teachers and parents use competition as a way to get kids to do something. We have sports events where the focus is entirely on winning, spelling bees which leave one winner and many losers, report cards with precise ranking, and many and frequent comparisons of one child with another. My sense of all this is that it does more harm than good. There are excellent examples from the corporate world where management movement from harsh competition to increased cooperation has done wonders for a bottom line. Functional leadership in the business world demands a high level of integration rather than the traditional hierarchies. Competition, or trying to beat the other person, becomes an end in itself, and gets in the way of the simple joy of achievement for its own sake. Competition is part of the win-lose aspect of the world, a zero sum game, where whatever one person gains the other loses, like being on a seesaw. For every winner there is a loser. Competition is not a motivator, although it can certainly change behavior, at least temporarily, and is a technique that schools and teachers sometimes use to control kids. As I will point out later, real motivation must come from within.

Further, competition is the diametric opposite of co-operation, and the ability to be cooperative is a sought-after skill in today's world where teamwork can be crucial to success. The Learn-to-Learn child should be more on the cooperative than the competitive end of the spectrum. If you doubt the negative effects of too much competition, recall the articles in newspapers recently about the incredible antics of some parents with respect to kids' sports.

• A man shouted profanities at a Little League baseball mom, and later punched the coach.

• In January 2002, a sideline father beat another man to death in the aftermath of a kids' hockey game.

• A town in New Jersey built a moat around a playing field to keep hyper-competitive parents at a distance.

Although a gentle kind of competition can be a fun part of a game, and even be useful, the most important parental role with respect to Learn to Learn is to soften the effects of competition for the child, making sure that the negative effects are minor, not debilitating, and that the real joy in learning comes from the learning itself, not from getting ahead of someone else.

With respect to this issue, here is what I can do to help my child:

41. Feedback/Evaluation

I sometimes find it useful to redefine a word or words to make a point, and I'm going to do it here to illustrate what I think is an important distinction. These words- feedback and evaluation - are often used interchangeably. But there is an important difference, especially from the perspective of Learn to Learn. Evaluation is the act of ap- plying a value - good or bad - to one's work. A grade on a report card or a paper or project is an example. Usually one person, the teacher in the case of grades, evaluates another, the child.

Feedback, on the other hand, is objective information given that is value free, leaving the receiver of the feed- back to apply the "good" or "bad" to it. So I can say to you about this handbook for example, "I'd like to have lots of feedback, but, based on your feedback and that of others, I'll do my own evaluating".

Feedback stays in the control of the receiver, who can use it or not. If he uses it, it becomes his own and can be a powerful tool for growth. As a university teacher, I sought feedback both during the course that I taught and at the end of the course, using a form to elicit my students' re-actions to class exercises or other activities. As a result, I would change the format of the course the next time I taught it, adding more activities like the ones they found instructive and useful, and deleting the ones that their feedback said were not useful.

Grades on a report card, incidentally, are primarily evaluation, and a rather poor form of feedback. They are much too simplistic, and much too evaluative. For this reason I suggest you not pay too much attention to your child's grades, good or bad, and rather help him to be a seeker of feedback. If your child is not sure what a given grade means, encourage him to ask the teacher to be more specific, and how he could do better, in the teacher's opinion, next time.

Feedback is most useful if it is given immediately af-ter the behavior, sought rather than given without being asked, if it is non-judgemental, specific, and is something over which the child has control.

Try to increase the feedback you provide for your child, and decrease the evaluation. Try to model the seeking of feedback, so that the child can become comfortable with asking, "Daddy, how do you think I did?". If your own ego can be submerged a bit, you might even try asking your child for feedback! "Bobby, how did I do in helping you figure out how to do that assignment?

With respect to this issue, here is what I can do to help my child:

42. Systems Thinking

It goes without saying that issues of importance in today's complex world - from personal to interpersonal to international - are highly complex, infinitely nuanced; surely not black and white, nor good and evil. They demand for their solution similarly complex thinking skills. The world is a system, and more than lineal thinking is required to solve problems.

Several years ago, I visited a seventh grade science classroom, taught by a brilliant young teacher. The theme was systems, and I found the curriculum and the teaching dynamic and exciting. The children viewed a wonderful film, which described how a farmer dammed up a stream in order to provide power, through a water wheel, to grind his grain. But the dammed up stream created ecological changes that affected the fields where the grain was grown, and a chain of events caused extensive problems. The point was that factor A can influence factor B, which then influences factor C, which can in turn go back to influence factor A. The teacher used the film as a model for many other systems, and helped the seventh graders to develop skills in a much more complex fashion. The kids were really turned on. If only the world's political leaders were aware of systems, and could think in more than a lineal fashion!

The program was expanded, and now many schools are using the systems idea to help kids think about more complex and dynamic situations. A wonderful organization, the Waters Foundation, has been established and supports the idea. Here is a quote from their web site.

Dynamic systems predominate in the world. Understanding dynamic systems is crucial to successful learning and living. Demonstrated understanding of dynamic systems is an integral part of local, state, and national standards in many curricular areas. Using concepts and tools of systems thinking/dynamic modeling allows students to develop and demonstrate understanding of dynamic systems.

For over ten years now, K-12 educators have been utilizing systems thinking/dynamic modeling in classrooms across the United States. Applications vary greatly and have been implemented in many areas of the curriculum and at every grade level. No matter the topic or the age of the students, reports of success are consistent. What is the basis for these enthusiastic reports? Is it the use of technology? Students certainly enjoy the unique use of computers. However, the attention to task and the learning results seem to occur even in connected activities that do not require the computer.

Exploration of dynamic complexity is a highly motivating learning experience for students. Their learning is enhanced by the "real" nature of the problems that they explore and the sense that they are developing skills that will prove useful throughout their lives. The merging of system dynamics and the characteristics of effective instruction creates tremendous potential for engaging students in powerful learning experiences.

Research shows that instructional settings that optimize learning should be student-centered, experiential, holistic, and authentic. In addition, students should be provided opportunities to utilize many forms of expression, to reflect, to interact with other students, and to collaborate. Learning should be developmental and should involve the construction of ideas and systems. Effective applications of systems thinking/dynamic modeling include all of these characteristics. What appears to be most successful is an essential combination of the powerful concepts and tools of system dynamics with best practice in instructional strategies.

An interesting book is listed on the web site, "When a Butterfly Sneezes", by Linda Booth Sweeney. The subtitle is "A Guide for Helping Kids Explore Interconnections in Our World Through Favorite Stories". It describes ways to help children become systems thinkers through stories, and is a delightful, loving book. An endorsement by Peter Senge, author of "The Fifth Discipline", a marvelous systems book, and a Professor at MIT says "Thanks to this wonderful guidebook, parents can now join the growing number of educators in developing children's innate capacities for systems thinking. Help your children discover the systems lessons in many of their favorite stories and explore together a way of thinking about our lives as in-terrelated with one another and with nature".

Systems thinking is a classic example of Learning to Learn.

The Waters Foundation web site can be found at www.watersfoundation.org "When a Butterfly Sneezes" is listed by Amazon.com

With respect to this issue, here is what I can do to help my child:

43. Vocational Education as Learning to Learn

I've often been impressed with the amazing teaching competence of many vocational education teachers. They come from the ranks of the discipline itself, such as auto body work, or TV repair or whatever. They are often wonderful teachers, because a hands-on approach is native to them. It's the way they learned, rather than being taught by an expert. They learned the skills of learning and how to become a self-learner. If your child is in a vocational program, you can be especially helpful by supporting the hands-on idea; starting the sequence of learning with an experience, a "Why don't you try it" time, and then helping them to analyze the results and figure out how it went.

The modern vocational-technical high school, in courses in automotive technology, helps students to be expert diagnosticians, using logic to quickly and accurately find the exact problem.

You can use the "hands on" method yourself, when you show your child how to use a toothbrush, the telephone, a vacuum cleaner, a paint brush, the lawn mower, or even a computer. Let him give it a try, experiment with it a bit, allowing your youngster to learn from his mistakes and successes. Of course you should try not to let frustration get in the way; a bit of gentle support is always in order. But try to leave the major exploration to the child.

You also might consider taking your child with you to work for a day to see how you deal with issues that arise and how you solve problems.

With respect to this issue, here is what I can do to help my child:

44. Reading

Reading is a twin to listening as a tool for learning. Imagine your life if you did not know how to read or if you could not read well or even if you didn't like to read. And if you are one of the few adults who don't really like to read, think how your life could be richer and more fulfilling if you did have that wonderful love of reading.

By far, the biggest part of helping a child to read well is your attitude toward learning in general, and reading in particular. It is a certainty that if you are a good reader, enjoy reading, and love to learn from reading, that same set of skills and attitudes will be imbued in your child. If, on the other hand, you do not model reading or at least the love of reading, you and your child both have a problem.

Of all the skills learned in school, it seems to me that reading is the least amenable to direct instruction. Sure, there are reading techniques to learn, and teaching reading demands a high level of teaching skill. But in my experience, actual reading instruction has precious little to do with how well a child eventually reads. Forget the silly argument between phonics or whole word instruction. To learn to read, a child needs to read. And to read, he needs to enjoy reading. It's almost that simple.

Here are a few ideas from my experience that should be of use to you in seeing that your child becomes a competent reader.

• Model reading and a love for reading. Read yourself, and make it clear to your child how much you enjoy and learn from reading. But don't put on any pressure.

• Tell your child about the books and magazines you read, what the novels were about, how exciting a mystery book was, what interesting things you learned from the nonfiction, and what it meant to you.

• Check out libraries and especially bookstores with your child. Libraries often have great programs to help kids love to learn, and modern libraries are far from stuffy. Bookstores are now very "cool" places, and there is every reason for children to love to visit a bookstore. Try to set your priorities such that there is always money to buy a book or magazine, and if not, make good use of the library.

• Be sure that your child owns some books. Books make a fine present, but giving him the money to make his own selection might be even better than you deciding what book would be good for him. Content is only a part of the issue. Just plain reading, regardless of the content, is very worthwhile. And be sure that he has a bookcase of his own in his bedroom.

• Here's a no-no. Don't be coercive to get a child to read more or better. Let him learn to love reading as you do, and it will flow by itself. Reading needs to be fun to be productive.

• Remember that there is extensive reading on a computer screen and in magazines and comic books, even the backs of cereal boxes.

• Again, be sure you model reading and the love of reading yourself!

With respect to this issue, here is what I can do to help my child:

45. Motivation

Motivation is an often misunderstood phenomenon. Some years ago, a researcher studied the concept in relation to management. The question was "How can a manager motivate the workers". It seems that the question would have a set of easily identifiable answers, centered on rewards and punishments. But the research showed a very interesting distinction, which is highly applicable to the parental role. The basic point is that one person - parent, teacher, friend - cannot really motivate another person. You can indeed influence the other person's behavior with rewards and punishment, for example, but real motivation comes from within. A child can motivate himself, but a parent can not motivate the child. If you have ever tried to lose weight or quit smoking you are fully aware that the desire for change - the motivation - has to come from within for any program to really work.

What you as a parent can do is set the stage for the child's motivation or at the very least, avoid getting in the way. Specifically, you can help a child to find the joy in learning, understand the rewards that the child has brought upon himself by working hard at school. See that he takes the credit, not the rules or rewards that you have imposed. If you have lost weight through the Weight Watcher's program, you should take the credit yourself, not give all the credit to the program. You did the hard part! Do your best to see that the pleasures of learning are internal, not provided by you or the school. The pleasure derived from a good report card only makes sense if it is a reflection of the true joy of learning.

There are surely some rewards that you can supply, like a fun trip to a ball game or museum, or especially your own admiration and respect for your child, but provide them for their own sake rather than as a reward for an "A".

In summary, help your child to be a self-motivator rather than providing the rewards and punishment yourself.

With respect to this issue, here is what I can do to help my child:

46. Outlining

One of the most useful exercises I ever undertook was in a freshman English class in college. The professor wanted us to plan a well organized paper, and started with the idea of an outline. He handed each of us in the class an envelope with perhaps 20 or 30 strips of paper, each with a phrase or sentence. He told us it was an outline of an article, cut up into strips, but without the headings of I, II, III, or A, B, C. We were to arrange them into four levels, some with Roman numerals, some with upper case letters, some with arabic numerals, some with lower case letters. (I., A., 1., a.) We were to arrange the strips in the right order. It only took a few minutes, but the exercise taught me a lot about how to organize something I was about to write, or even speak. I still outline almost everything I write, so that it will be organized, and one idea leads smoothly into the next. As a teacher in later years, whenever I read a student's paper, I was aware how much better the paper was if it flowed from an outline. Too often, it seemed that a student just sat down and started at the beginning with no particular plan, adding an idea as it occurred to him, often making strange jumps from one idea to another, and sometimes going in circles. I kept wanting to correct the paper by using scissors and tape!

One very simple plan for a paper is:
I. Introduction
II. The body of the paper
  A. First major point
  B. Second major point
  C. Third major point
III. Conclusion

Most word processing programs have an outline feature which can help.

There is an excellent computer program called Inspiration 7.0, used in some schools, which gives templates for outlines, making organizing a paper almost as simple as filling in the blanks. The Learn to Learn part is that kids can see the logic entailed, and move toward clearer thinking. This in turn forms the basis for more complex thinking and understanding of patterns. And it's all a great way for parents to get involved. Maybe you could even use the cut-up outline trick yourself!

With respect to this issue, here is what I can do to help my child:

47. Parents' Expectations

The popular press has recently centered on the importance of high expectations for students on the part of parents and schools. Parents with high expectations for their children seem to have youngsters that indeed do better, who are able to meet those expectations. I suspect that if the expectations are set too high, however, or too much attention is paid to the parents' expectations, there could be a backlash - a child who is frustrated by never being able to quite meet the expectations. Still, if reasonable, expectations can form a useful guide for a child.

But the important aspect of expectations or standards, the most permanent and functional part, is helping the child set his own standards, develop his own expectations for himself. Check out your own situation. Do you work harder and smarter, and thus do better, if you are trying to meet someone else's standards for you, or if you are working to meet your own standards? Maybe that's a tough question; maybe it's different at different times or in different circumstances, but my bet is on the long term usefulness of a person working on his own standards rather than someone else's.

If this makes sense to you with respect to your child, try to engage the child in setting goals, establishing expectations, defining standards. At the end of a given quarter at school, for example, ask your child what his plans are for the next quarter. Without pressure, ask what he will try to accomplish, what his goals are for the next three months, or even the next three days? A useful question for a child when he is planning his goals is "How will you know when you have been successful?" This helps him to establish criteria, so that the satisfaction is more likely to happen, and will be seen as a direct result of the planning. Be supportive of the child's own goal setting rather than setting the goals for him. In the long run, you'll be glad you did, and so will your child.

With respect to this issue, here is what I can do to help my child:

48. Support for Teachers

Teachers are without question the lifeblood of American education. Underpaid, overworked, often selfless, caring, service oriented people who have undertaken the staggeringly difficult job of teaching America's' youth. They deserve our almost complete support.

Almost???

There is a caveat. Let's keep a sense of balance. Children indeed must respect their teachers, and realize that the teacher is the boss. But I harbor memories from when I was a kid that give me pause as I write this. My mother was such a complete supporter of my teachers - so concerned that I be a "good boy", and do whatever the teacher wanted - that I quickly realized that I was a mere pawn in the equation. I recall several instances when I knew that the teacher was not right, either in factual information or in the way she dealt with me or with other kids - but my mother sided with the teacher simply because she was the teacher. My mother believed in absolute authority. There was no chance that my views had any meaning if they were contrary to the teachers' views. I learned about justice and hierarchies very early, and not all the learning was functional.

Indeed parents must support the teacher and the school system; and it is quite real that the teacher is and should be the boss. But maintain balance. You need to be supportive of your child too!

With respect to this issue, here is what I can do to help my child:

49. Help Your Child to be an Independent Thinker

A few months ago I was contemplating buying a digital camera. Since I knew that a good friend of mine had one, and knew a lot about photography, I asked for his advice on which one to buy. I also did a lot of research on the internet, through computer magazines and in stores.

My friend told me which one to buy; the same one he had and enjoyed. I considered his points carefully, but I decided on a different one, which I felt represented a better value and was more consistent with my own criteria, including price. My friend, I discovered from his wife, was really upset with me. "Why", he had said, "did he ask me if he didn't want to do what I said!!" He was apparently upset that I considered him one of several resources available to me, and that I would decide for myself which camera to buy.

My mother was a great believer in experts, as proven by credentials. It would never have occurred to her to question in the slightest what her doctor told her to do. "He's a doctor; he's an expert; he's right". She would be appalled if she knew of the interactions I have with my doctor. I ask him for information, he provides it as best he can, sometimes refers me to another person or resource for additional data, and suggests alternatives. But he is very sensitive to knowing that I want to be in control of my own health, and he respects that. He is an expert, but his expertise is tempered by an understanding of his patients' needs to assemble all the information and make their own decisions, not simply do what the expert says.

It's not just that "Johnny said..." or "The teacher said..." or "The book said..." or even "My mother said..."

Being an independent thinker is especially crucial today, as more and more of our media is from conglomerates; TV stations, radio and newspapers all owned by the same corporation. Independent thinkers seek multiple resources, and learn to be critical without being cynical.

My point is that it is good to help your child be an independent thinker, to use multiple sources of information and his own feelings and intuition, to apply his own criteria and to come to his own decisions. Being an independent learner is a sign of maturity, and an important aspect of learning to learn.

With respect to this issue, here is what I can do to help my child:

50. Planning

Curriculum developers often use a three stage pattern to plan the material they want used in schools. It's an excellent pattern, and one that I suggest that you use, but it's unfortunate that children are not more involved in planning their own instruction. If they were, the material would be more relevant, and much more motivating. The three stages are: Objectives, Activities, and Evaluation. You can use this pattern with your child to plan a learning sequence, or, for that matter, anything you and your child want to do. Use the pattern to ask questions, then "fill in the blanks" with your child's responses.

A diagram of the pattern would look like this:

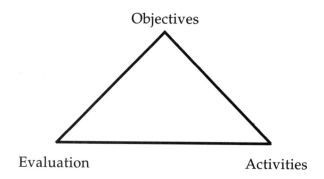

Objectives

Evaluation   Activities

The first step is determining objectives. Be careful, because objectives are not something one does, but rather the desired outcome of what one does. It seems a bit backwards, but you should start with the outcomes in order to make sense of the activities. Curriculum designers try to make the objectives as behavioral and as specific as possible, and always future oriented. An example might be "By next Thursday I'll be able to give a presentation in my science class about marsupials, have the teacher compliment me, and be able to say truthfully I had fun doing it."

The second stage is to plan the activities that he can undertake to accomplish that objective. Your child might suggest things like:

"I'll read the section on marsupials in the encyclopedia at school and write down important information.

"I'll check out marsupial and maybe some examples of marsupials on the net, and print out copies of any pictures or other interesting things I can find."

"I'll go to the zoo Tuesday afternoon to see what examples there are there, and take notes.

"On Wednesday, I'll write an outline of my talk, including adding some pictures that I'll take at the zoo. Then I'll try out the talk with my father Wednesday night."

The final phase, and one that's very important, is evaluation. How can your child tell if the objectives were met? It pays to review the objectives and talk about how it went. What did the teacher say? Did other kids comment? Did it inspire some discussion? Did you have fun doing it? And most of all, be sure to ask your child "How did <u>you</u> feel about it?"

With some practice, the evaluation can even be used to determine which activities were most important in accomplishing the objectives, and which the least. Then next time a similar activity is undertaken, there will be a base of experience to call upon.

With respect to this issue, here is what <u>I</u> can do to help <u>my</u> child:

Develop Your Own

So there you have it. Fifty nifty ways to help your child learn how to learn.

I am fully aware, of course, that many of these are not directly applicable to your child or your situation, or even to your values. Hopefully there are many that do connect directly for you and are immediately useful.

The most important concept you can take from this simple handbook is the general idea of learning how to learn, and an understanding of the Learn to Learn pattern, so that you can design your own specific techniques, maybe even intuitively moving in a Learn-to-Learn supportive direction.

The basic pattern is deductive learning, specifically illustrated by the EAT concept, which I explored with you in No. 18. You might now re-read that one, review any notes you wrote after each of the fifty, and think of ways in which you can develop your own techniques for use with your own child, using the EAT pattern.

And to be a true Learn to Learn parent supporter, do it in conjunction with your child, so that you and your child are colleagues in the learning process.

Join the Learn to Learn Forum

The idea of Learning to Learn is gaining interest all over the world. The concept has exciting potential, not only for improving learning for schools and children, but also for important social and political change.

I have developed a simple web site devoted to the L2L concept, which includes an interactive forum.

Please join the web site, read the comments of others, and add your thoughts. What do you think of the Learn to Learn idea? What have you tried with your child? How did it work? How does your child react? What did not work? What questions or suggestions do you have for other participants in the forum?

The address is:
www.learningtolearn.org

We are looking forward to hearing from you!